WHAT'S YOUR SCORING AVERAGE ON THESE TWO-POINT QUESTIONS?

- Who are the two repeaters from last years NBA Coaches All Defensive Team?

- Who are: Pistol Pete? Clyde? The Hawk? Dollar Bill? The Pearl? Mr. Clutch?

- What did Bailey Howell, Larry Siegfried, Emmette Bryant, Don May, Bill Hosket, and Mike Warren all have in common at the end of last season?

- Which NBA team placed two freshmen on the league's All-Rookie team? Who are they?

- Which pro owns the record for most points scored in the NBA? Which pro holds the record for most points scored in a three-year major-college career?

If your scoring total isn't 100 percent, it will be after you're read these and many other fascinating facts in

BASKETBALL STARS OF 1971

LOUIS SABIN, Articles Editor
of *Boys' Life* magazine, is the
author of numerous magazine articles,
books, and crossword puzzles. He lives with
his wife, Francene, and son, Keith, age seven,
in East Brunswick, New Jersey.

BASKETBALL
STARS
OF 1971

LOUIS SABIN

PYRAMID BOOKS • NEW YORK

For Francene, who leads my career in assists

BASKETBALL STARS OF 1971
A PYRAMID BOOK

First printing, October 1970

PYRAMID BOOKS are published by Pyramid Publications
A Division of The Walter Reade Organization, Inc.
444 Madison Avenue, New York, New York 10022, U.S.A.

CONTENTS

The Season Past

Individual players stood out for different reasons in the 1969-70 season, but for sheer brilliance and pure basketball beauty the glory of the New York Knickerbockers is the story of the season past. They came out of the starting gate a cohesive group of ballplayers drilled and disciplined in the fine art of team play, racing away from every club they met as they piled up a huge lead over the rest of the Eastern Division. Included in that breakaway start was an 18-game winning streak, and it wasn't until the latter part of the season that the Knicks relaxed and let the rest of the NBA win a few at their expense. The Knick lapse benefited the Milwaukee Bucks the most, as the Alcindor-led squad closed strongly enough to take second place in the East and show that they would present an even stronger challenge in 1970-71.

By playoff time, though, the New Yorkers had regained the smoothness that had carried them to a 60-22 won-lost season. It was a good thing they did, because the third-place Baltimore Bullets were out to revenge last season's playoffs, when the Knicks wiped them off the court in four straight. With Gus Johnson, Wes Unseld and Earl Monroe playing inspired ball, the Knicks were pressed right down to the seventh game before they could continue their run for the title.

Next came the Bucks, but strong Knick defense stopped Alcindor from destroying them single-handedly, and the rest of the Milwaukee squad failed to come through. The result was a fairly easy Knick conquest in five games.

Meanwhile, in the West the Lakers were playing Dr. Jekyl and Mr. Hyde. With Wilt Chamberlain back in the lineup after missing most of the season because of a torn tendon in his right knee, Los Angeles figured to romp over Connie Hawkins and the Phoenix Suns. Instead, they had to battle back from a 3-1 deficit to take three straight from Phoenix for the opportunity to face the tough Atlan-

7

ta Hawks, winners of the Western Division regular season title. But the Hawks played like birds with broken wings and L.A. downed them in four straight.

For the Lakers it was the seventh time they were going after the NBA title. For the Knicks it was the first time they had reached the finals in 17 years, and no New York team had ever been kings of the NBA. Game One was staged at New York's Madison Square Garden, in front of the usual sellout crowd of 19,500 fans. New York was too much for Chamberlain, West and Baylor, taking an easy 124-112 contest. Game Two was tight from start to finish, with the Lakers edging by the Knicks in the last seconds, 105-103.

The scene shifted to the Forum for the next two contests. But even though Jerry West hit on a fantastic 60-foot desperation shot with two seconds left, to send the game into overtime, the Knicks came out strong and steady, grabbing a 2-1 series lead with a 111-108 win. Title play continued to seesaw as the Lakers bounced back in Game Four, with Jerry West scoring 37 points and picking up 18 assists to spearhead the Lakers' 121-115 victory.

So the road show returned to New York for Game Five. It turned out to be the pivotal game of the series when, even though Reed had to leave with a badly strained hip muscle and New York behind 25-15 in the first quarter, the Knicks outran, outmaneuvered and outdefensed a seemingly helpless L.A. squad to come out on top, 107-100. Nobody within hearing or sight of the game could have believed it possible that the Knicks—at such a distinct height disadvantage and with their high-scoring center unavailable to struggle against the titanic Chamberlain—could even stay in the game, much less win it. Everyone was stunned by the outcome—the Knicks, their delirious fans, and the entire Laker team, now facing the end of everything as the two teams flew back to Los Angeles for the sixth game.

Back home, the Lakers regrouped and with Chamberlain overwhelming all the bodies Red Holzman put in the game to contain him to pour in 45 points and snare 27 rebounds, the game ended L.A. 135, N.Y. 113. Reed watched the slaughter in civilian clothes, sharing his teammates' fears that he wouldn't even be able to take the floor for the seventh and deciding game. But a combination of medical treatment and his own sheer guts enabled him to join his team on the Garden floor in time for the opening tap-off. His presence was all the Knicks needed to lift them to the heights, and although he scored only two baskets and was dragging his bad leg back and forth for virtually the entire first half, the Knicks took the crown with a flair, downing L.A. 113-99.

Jerry West and Elgin Baylor, despite fine performances by both, went home still not knowing what it feels like to rule the NBA. Willis Reed had the feeling and loved it, along with the car presented him by *Sport* Magazine as the series' outstanding player.

Outstanding in another way was the continuation of the struggle between the NBA and ABA to acquire the services of the nation's best college ballplayers—even though it was a recognized fact that the two leagues would eventually merge. The two best collegiate stars were Pete Maravich of LSU—a fancy passer and hot-shooting backcourt prospect—and St. Bonaventure's Bob Lanier. The Atlanta Hawks corraled Maravich for a contract that was reportedly worth 1.9-million dollars. The 6'-11" Lanier was grabbed by the Detroit Pistons, hungry for that goooood big man to solve their problems. Other notable NBA acquisitions were Rudy Tomjanovich, of Michigan, selected by San Diego; Dave Cowens, of Florida State, picked by the Boston Celtics; and Ralph Ogden, of Santa Clara, taken by San Francisco.

Strengthened by an outstanding crop of college standouts, the teams then had to make available players for the expansion draft to stock the three new entries into the league: the Buffalo Braves, Cleveland Cavaliers, and Portland Trail Blazers. Los Angeles left their fine rookie, Dick Garrett, unprotected. Buffalo snatched him immediately. Surprisingly, the Knicks lost only Bill Hosket, Don May and John Warren, although regulars Mike Riordan, Dave Stallworth and Dick Barnett figured to be in the list of unprotected New Yorkers. Another surprise was that Boston gave up Larry Siegfried, who was chosen by Portland and immediately traded to San Diego.

To accommodate the newcomers, the NBA Board of Governors approved a four-division alignment of teams for this year's 82-game schedule. This season's divisional breakdown is: ATLANTIC DIVISION—Boston Celtics, Buffalo Braves, New York Knickerbockers, Philadelphia 76ers; CENTRAL DIVISION—Atlanta Hawks, Baltimore Bullets, Cincinnati Royals, Cleveland Cavaliers; MIDWEST DIVISION—Chicago Bulls, Detroit Pistons, Milwaukee Bucks, Phoenix Suns; PACIFIC DIVISION—Los Angeles Lakers, Portland Trail Blazers, San Diego Rockets, San Francisco Warriors, Seattle SuperSonics.

Another note that was sounded was the trade of Oscar Robertson to Milwaukee for Flynn Robinson and returning serviceman Charlie Paulk. It was no secret that Robertson would be leaving Cincinnati for somewhere, as he and Royals coach Bob Cousy had been at odds all season long and one deal, that would have sent Oscar to Baltimore in exchange for Gus Johnson, was nixed by the Big O during the season. Another swap took place when Chicago sent Clem Haskins to Phoenix for Jim Fox and a draft choice.

The regular season of NBA play produced its usual list of leaders, which included some expected results and a few unexpected ones. The 1969-70 schedule ended with these men on top: Jerry West took scoring-average honors, based on 2,309 points in 74 games, for a 31.2 ppg mark, although Lew Alcindor—who placed second—had 2,361 points in 82 games; veteran Johnny Green of Cincinnati had the best field-goal percentage, .559; Flynn Robinson's free-throw percentage of .898 led the way in that department; Elvin Hayes took the rebound title on the basis of 1,386 caroms and a 16.9 average; and head player in the assists race was Seattle's player-coach, Len Wilkens, with 683 assists and a 9.1 per-game breakdown.

Rookie of the Year was a runaway for Big Lew Alcindor, who brought the Bucks from a last-place finish in 1969 to a second place slot last year. Another deserving award went to Willis Reed as he was named the league's Most Valuable Player. Rounding out the All-Rookie Team with Alcindor were: his Milwaukee teammate, Bob Dandridge; JoJo White, of Boston; Dick Garrett, of the Lakers (and now Buffalo); and Baltimore's Mike Davis (also of Buffalo).

The NBA All-Star First Team was made up of center Willis Reed; guards Jerry West and Walt Frazier; and forwards Billy Cunningham (Philadelphia), and Gus Johnson. The second Team was comprised of Alcindor, Connie Hawkins (Phoenix), John Havlicek (Boston), Oscar Robertson, and Lou Hudson (Atlanta).

The NBA All-Defensive Team, initiated last year, was rightfully loaded with Knicks. The 1970 five who were chosen were: Willis Reed, Dave DeBusschere and Walt Frazier, all of New York, and Gus Johnson and Jerry West. Second to them in the voting were Havlicek, Alcindor, Atlanta's Joe Caldwell and Bill Bridges, and Chicago's Jerry Sloan.

Red Holzman was designated Coach of the Year for the magnificent job he did blending the Knicks into a devastating court combination. He received 17 of the 40 votes cast.

Next came L.A.'s Joe Mullaney, with nine votes, followed by Atlanta's Richie Guerin and Milwaukee's Larry Costello (five each), Dick Motta of Chicago (3), and Len Wilkens of Seattle (1).

Over in the American Basketball Association, Los Angeles and Indiana met for the championship, with Indiana taking it. Other ABA champs, on the basis of individual effort, were: Spencer Haywood, who scored the most points (2,519) and had the best scoring average (29.9). He also grabbed the most rebounds (1,637) and had the best rebounding average (19.4). Along the way he broke Connie Hawkins' single-game ABA scoring record by netting 59 points. And by season's end he was named both Rookie of the Year and Most Valuable Player. Along with the 59-point standard, the 6-9 Denver star set new ABA highs in total points, total rebounds and rebounding average. Kentucky Colonel Darel Carrier also won two honors: best in free-throw average (.892), and 3-point field goals (105 on 280 attempts, for a .375 mark). His teammate, Louie Dampier, led the league in most 3-pointers for the second year, with 198. Washington's Larry Brown topped his own record in playmaking with 580 assists in 82 games, for a 7.07 average. His teammate, Frank Card, won the 2-point field-goal crown with a .530 average.

The ABA All-Star Team's first five were: Spencer Haywood and Larry Jones (Denver); Rick Barry (Washington); Mel Daniels (Indiana); and Bob Verga (Carolina).

The second team was made up of: Roger Brown and Bob Netolicky (Indiana); Red Robbins (New Orleans); Louie Dampier (Kentucky); and Don Freeman (Miami).

THE SEASON PRESENT

Atlantic Division

NEW YORK KNICKERBOCKERS: Last season the team that calls Madison Square Garden home squared off against all comers from the outset and won, won, won. Their success was grounded in defense—a thing of beauty and a joy to behold—under the masterful direction of Coach of the Year Red Holzman. And this season promises more of the same.

The expansion draft at year's end didn't hurt the Knicks a bit; in fact, it made room for returnee Phil Jackson, the hard-nosed forward who sat out 1969-70 to fully recuperate from an operation; and a fine crop of rookies will enable Holzman to fill the gaps created by the loss of Don May, Bill Hosket, Nate Bowman and John Warren to expansion teams.

This year's team could staff an all-star squad, starting with MVP Willis Reed at center, scorer-playmaker-defensive-genius Walt Frazier in the backcourt, and scorer-rebounder-defense-minded Dave DeBusschere in the forecourt. It continues with "Dollar" Bill Bradley, Dick Barnett, Cazzie Russell; then Dave Stallworth and Mike Riordan, who flow in and out of the lineup to meet the needs of every moment.

A full season of playing as a fluid unit has only added more confidence (if that's possible) to a team that won 60 games to lead the Eastern Division in '70. Included in their run for the money was a record-smashing 18-game win streak, which helped convince virtually all doubters that New York had indeed founded a dynasty that could, in time, rival the great Celtic era.

With the new alignment of teams, the Knicks are far and away the best of the Atlantic Division. Only the wrath of the gods—in the form of injuries—can stop them from being No. 1.

PHILADELPHIA 76ERS: Coach Jack Ramsay's boys just managed to get past the .500 mark last year to finish a poor fourth in the East. Their outstanding weapon was All-Star Billy Cunningham, the hot-shooting forward who will again bolster the 76er attack this year unless he has another change of mind about where he wants to play—in Philadelphia for the NBA or for the Carolina Cougars of the ABA.

They lost George Wilson and Fred Hetzel in the expansion draft but picked up some rebounding help in a trade that brought veteran Bailey Howell to the club. And rookie Dennis Awtrey, from Santa Clara, may give them more muscle in the rebounding department.

Otherwise, it is essentially the same squad that was trounced by the Bucks in the playoffs. Hustle is the name of their game, a necessary attitude when you have to compensate for lack of height and not quite the right ingredients that make a "short" team like the Knicks such a devastating force.

Billy the Kid is Philly's big gun. Cunningham scored at a 26.1 ppg pace last year and pulled down 1,101 rebounds. Behind him in 76er scoring were Hal Greer, with a 22.0 scoring average, and Archie Clark, with a 19.7 ppg average. Greer is still a fine all-around floor man, although age is a factor as he enters his 12th pro season. The expected return to health of Luke Jackson did not materialize, and his 37 games' contribution was a thorough disappointment to Philadelphia hopefuls. If he can come back this year, the team's prospects improve considerably because he can take some rebounding weight off the shoulders of others, who would then be freer to think about scoring and playmaking. As it was, Darrall Imhoff and Jim Washington were the only players able to give Cunningham any real assistance going to the boards.

With rebounding punch, Philly could improve vastly this season, for there are six scoring threats on the squad: Cunningham, Greer, Clark, Imhoff, Washington, and Wally Jones. Otherwise, the 76ers can hope for nothing more than a weak second-place finish in a division ruled by the Knicks.

BOSTON CELTICS: Trailing clouds of glory, the Celtics face another season prepared to trail along behind their betters. For without a Bill Russell at center, they are just another bunch of players.

They won't be a complete wipe-out because they can field 1) the inexhaustible John Havlicek, who last season led the team in scoring (1,960 points and a 24.2 ppg average), rebounds (635), and minutes played (3,369). More than ever, his pride and hustle will keep the team from falling flat on its face; 2) JoJo White, whose freshman debut earned him All-Rookie Team selection; and Don Nelson, who was Boston's No. 2 scorer (15.4 ppg) and a solid all-around player.

Henry Finkel is not the center they were hoping would step into Bill Russell's sneakers, and top draft pick Dave Cowens (Florida State) will get a close look when he reports to training camp. So will Rex Morgan, Jacksonville's dynamic backcourt general.

The rebuilding goes on as Boston gets set to settle for third spot.

BUFFALO BRAVES: The expansion club snared a couple of good starters in the draft when they acquired Dick Garrett of Los Angeles (a member of 1970's All-Rookie First Team) and Mike Davis, another fine rookie who played for Baltimore last year and made the All-Rookie squad.

The Braves' greatest strength is in having the services of Eddie Donovan as general manager. Donovan, more than anybody else, was responsible for putting together the current Knickerbocker ensemble.

Unless they indulge in trades between now and the season's opener, their roster will be: Garrett, Davis, Ray Scott (from Baltimore), Nate Bowman, Mike Sillihan, Bill Hosket and Don May (from New York), Bob Kauffman (Philadelphia), Fred Crawford (Milwaukee), Herm Gilliam (Cincinnati), George Wilson (Philadelphia), Emmette Bryant (Boston), Mike Lynn (L.A.), and Paul Long (Detroit).

Central Division

ATLANTA HAWKS: As formidable a club as Richie Guerin had last year, this one is even better. Defense played a large part in the Hawks leading the Western Division in '70, and '71 should be more of the same. And the offense is nothing to sneer at either, with Lou Hudson a 25.4 ppg scorer last year and Joe Caldwell a 21.1 shooter.

If Guerin can continue to get the best out of much-traveled Walt Bellamy, Atlanta is set at center. And even though the Hawks lost Butch Beard and Don Ohl in the expansion draft, they are well stocked with backcourt players in Hudson, Walt Hazzard and Pistol Pete Maravich. It is Maravich who will bear special watching, because he and Hudson could provide Atlanta with the most prolific scoring tandem in NBA history. And even if Maravich doesn't hit at the tempo he maintained at LSU, his passing and playmaking could furnish the Hawks with a fantastic quarterback. Another addition from the college ranks is UCLA's John Vallely, who promises to become a regular in bunny-quick time.

Between Bellamy and Bill Bridges Atlanta's rebound totals should be mighty impressive, since each can be counted on to take away at least 1,000 caroms each. And with Jimmy Davis chipping in his share of boardwork, the team's fine shooters will be getting the ball with regularity.

All this balance and strength signals first place for the Hawks. And with Pistol Pete in the lineup, it signals a fine show when Atlanta's in town.

BALTIMORE BULLETS: The boys of Gene Shue don't have to look above them in the standings to see where the Knicks are, since New York isn't in their division. Instead, their uplifted eyes will find Atlanta where the Knicks used to be. That's only to say that Atlanta is that good, because Baltimore has the horses to give them a good race in the Central section. The Bullets lost Ray Scott and Leroy Ellis in the expansion raid, two men who could get rebounds: Scott had 457 last year and Ellis had 376. But Shue still has mighty Wes Unseld, second in the league carom race last year with 1,370, and muscular Gus Johnson, a bear off the boards who grabbed 1,086 rebounds in '69-70, along with Jack Marin (537 rebounds last year).

The shooting marks of this team are also formidable. Earl Monroe's final figures in '70 were 1,922 points and 23.4 ppg; Kevin Loughery had 1,207 and 21.9; Marin had

1,618 and 19.7; Johnson had 1,353 and 17.3; and Unseld had 1,325 and 16.2.

This is a hit-and-run team that never looked better than it did in the playoffs against the Knicks last year. If they can maintain the pace and spirit they showed against New York throughout that seven-game series, anything can happen. But over an 82-game schedule they just don't look capable of keeping pace with the Hawks.

CINCINNATI ROYALS: Herm Gilliam and Luther Rackley went in the draft, Jerry Lucas was traded away at the beginning of last year, and Oscar Robertson became a Milwaukee Buck in exchange for Charley Paulk and Flynn Robinson. So, as he promised, Coach Bob Cousy has begun his program of revamping the Royals in the hopes of getting together a crew that will play his kind of ball.

If it's shooting he wants, Flynn Robinson will give it to him, although the sharp-eyed Flynn won't give him the kind of defense a winning club needs. And rookie Sam Lacey has the look of a shooter, too. Another basket-conscious player on this club is Tom Van Arsdale, who hit for 1,621 points and a 22.8 ppg average last year.

The rest of the Royals can run and play with dash, but nobody looks capable of getting those all-important rebounds with any consistency. Paulk may prove helpful in this department, otherwise it's up to Johnny Green and Connie Dierking—which isn't too impressive.

So it's third place for the rebuilding Royals.

CLEVELAND CAVALIERS: Another aggregation of pickups (for which each expansion club paid $3.7 million), the Cavaliers snared a fine guard in Butch Beard from backcourt-rich Atlanta, and a reliable one in Johnny Egan, who appeared in the championship finals for Los Angeles. Another selection who could develop into a find is Johnny Warren, a rookie on last year's Knick roster. Otherwise, Cleveland's new entry into the NBA doesn't have the look of a multi-million-dollar baby. The rest of the squad consists of: Luther Rackley (Cincinnati), Walt Wesley (Chicago), Bobby Smith (San Diego), McCoy McLemore (Detroit), Len Chappell (Milwaukee), Bob Lewis (San Francisco), Don Ohl (Atlanta), and Loy Peterson (Chicago). A good college prospect is Dave Sorenson of Ohio State.

Midwest Division

MILWAUKEE BUCKS: Here they come, the new wave team that could make plenty of waves, and possibly even swamp every other club in the NBA. Only New York and Atlanta look superior, but with Oscar Robertson and Lew Alcindor mounting an inside-and-outside attack of awesome potential, this is definitely a team to be reckoned with.

What makes the Bucks less than the best is the rest of the squad behind the Big O and the Bigger L. John McGlocklin is a sharp backcourt man who can score—he hit 17.6 points per game last year—and move. Bob Dandridge came in just two points behind teammate Alcindor in the voting for the NBA All-Rookie Team, and he's a forward with a future. Greg and Don Smith showed potential to be even better than they were in '70, but they're "maybes."

The remainder of the roster is what makes Milwaukee an unknown factor. The Bucks picked up two good-looking college players in the draft: Gary Freeman (Oregon State) and John Rinka (Kenyon College).

It's the starting five that will carry the burden for this entry, but when two of that five are Alcindor and Robertson and the rest of the division consists of Phoenix, Chicago and Detroit, Milwaukee appears unstoppable.

PHOENIX SUNS: After Johnny Kerr stepped down as coach during the '70 season, the Suns responded to the persuasions of general manager Jerry Colangelo, who took over the reins. After finishing the regular season in a tie for third, the Suns came on like champions and just fell short of knocking L.A. out of the playoffs.

The biggest guns of last year were Connie Hawkins—a 24.6 ppg scorer who really impressed as an offensive weapon in his first NBA season, but who showed gaping weaknesses on defense; and Dick Van Arsdale—another pointmaker, who tallied at a 21.3 ppg rate last year. Joining them with their own fine set of credentials are 20.3-points-a-game Clem Haskins (acquired in a trade with Chicago in exchange for Jim Fox) and 7-1 Mel

Counts, a good outside shot (obtained from L.A. for Gail Goodrich). While Fox grabbed 570 rebounds last year, Haskins got 624 and Counts did even better with 683. And it will be up to Clem, Mel, Hawkins and Paul Silas to get the rebounds this year.

A good enough group, but a notch under Milwaukee.

CHICAGO BULLS: A fairly tough team, Chicago can field a professional front five but the bench doesn't come near to maintaining the standard.

Chet Walker is getting better and better. Last season saw him finish with a team-leading average of 21.5 points per game while lending a hand off the boards for 604 rebounds. Right behind him was Bob Love with 21.0 points a game and 712 rebounds. And the best player on the squad, Jerry Sloan, was hampered by injuries and appeared in only 53 games. A defensive star, Sloan scored at a 15.6 ppg clip in '70 and should do more this year.

Along with holdover Tom Boerwinkle, the services of Jim Fox (from Phoenix) will keep Chicago a solid rebounding threat, especially since a number of the boys are not board-shy.

The Bulls could be a second-place team instead of Phoenix, but they'll have to click all season long, stay happy and healthy, and get a few breaks along the way. The edge would seem to lie with Phoenix.

DETROIT PISTONS: On paper, the Pistons don't look like a team that should end up fourth in a four-team division. But along with talent, coach Bill van Breda Kolff has a number of question marks. Will the great college star, Bob Lanier of St. Bonaventure, prove as great a pro? The experts seem to think so, but they've been wrong before. How will Otto Moore react to playing forward and back-up center to Lanier after replacing Walt Bellamy at the pivot in '70? Will Jimmy Walker repeat his fine 21.0 points-per-game scoring, or will he fall back to what he was the previous two seasons? And Dave Bing, the consistently reliable scorer (22.9 ppg last year, to lead the team) —will he be in the game for Detroit or the ABA?

Put them all together and they spell ?????? And with so many uncertainties, Detroit seems to belong at the same position as a question mark—the end of the line.

Pacific Division

LOS ANGELES LAKERS: Like the Detroit Pistons, this is a team of question marks. But unlike the Pistons, there is enough material on this club to bring them home on top even if they suffer a couple of setbacks.

Wilt Chamberlain, whole and healthy, will be eyeing the championship again, not to mention the opportunity to add to his statistics as The Scorer. Jerry West is forever riding the carousel, reaching for the gold ring that would complete his otherwise illustrious career. Elgin Baylor is in the same boat as West: an all-time immortal who's never been on an NBA title team.

Aiding Joe Mullaney and the Big Three are a rugged cast of players. Keith Erickson came on strong in the '70 playoffs and really seems ready to keep it up. Rick Roberson showed he's no slouch at center (although Wilt goes to the bench only when he's hurt). John Tresvant and Happy Hairston are two more big plusses in the rebound department and can contribute in the scoring column as well—although West, Chamberlain and Baylor carry most of that load among them. Additional help should come from guard Gail Goodrich, a fine ball handler and 20.0 ppg scorer last year. Goodrich replaces Mel Counts in a trade with Phoenix.

As they were last season, L.A. is still mighty impressive, even though a mite on the old side. Before they retire, though, the Big Three can be counted on to win in the Pacific, and maybe—just maybe—astonish a lot of doubters by going all the way. We, for one, doubt it, but we'll give 'em the West Coast.

SAN FRANCISCO WARRIORS: The retirement of Nate Thurmond, announced last year after the classy center reinjured himself, is expected to be rescinded before this season gets underway. He's the key to the Warriors' hopes: with him they can go a long way up, without him the direction is reversed.

Without Thurmond, coach Al Attles can count these remaining blessings: Jeff Mullins, a sharpshooter who completed the '70 campaign with a 22.1 ppg average; Joe Ellis, who improved considerably last year and posted a

15.8 ppg average and chipped in with 594 rebounds; Jerry Lucas, still a powerful rebounder (906 in 63 games) and scorer (15.4 average for S.F. last year) even on a set of bad legs; Clyde Lee, good for 929 rebounds and an 11.0 ppg average last year. And more help should come from Ralph Ogden, the Warriors' second pick in the college draft. Also, Ron Williams continued to impress in his sophomore season, working the backcourt with Mullins, notching 424 assists (high on the club) and a 14.8 ppg average.

Look for the great Nate to bring S.F. home in second place in this division. Without him, though ...

SAN DIEGO ROCKETS: Selling Don Kojis to Seattle had to weaken the Rockets' attack but it may go a long way to restoring peace and unity to a team that lacked both last year. So, the Rockets come into '71 with their superstar Elvin Hayes leading the attack (he scored at a 27.5 ppg pace and rebounded 1,386 caroms last season). He'll get a fair share of help from John Block and Toby Kimball off the boards, and from ex-Celtic Larry Siegfried and college draftee Calvin Murphy in the scoring department. But the biggest asset to the team—after Hayes, of course—may well be muscular Rudy Tomjanovich, plucked off the Michigan campus. He can rebound and score, and if he transfers his college ability to the pros, he'll take a lot of weight off Hayes as the Rockets' all-purpose ballplayer.

San Diego doesn't look better than a third-place choice unless an impressive crop of rookies really comes through, in which case they could oust the Warriors from the second slot.

SEATTLE SUPERSONICS: Player-coach Lenny Wilkens is an excellent cager who got a lot out of his teammates in his debut as coach. But this is another first-five team that weakens quickly beyond the starting lineup. Along with Wilkens, Seattle can rely on Rob Rule, good for 825 rebounds and a 24.6 ppg average last year; Bob Boozer, who contributed 717 caroms and a 15.2 ppg mark; Don Kojis, a scorer, obtained from San Diego; Lucius Allen, who had a fair freshman year and should be better as a sophomore; a group of second-liners who play the game well enough to earn their pay but not much more.

Wilkens deserves better than this.

PORTLAND TRAIL BLAZERS: The third new entry into the NBA did reasonably well in the player draft, although they also didn't snare the most necessary item for success— a big center. Still, the Blazers won't look too bad fielding Rick Adelman and Jim Barnett (San Diego), Fred Hetzel (Philadelphia), Leroy Ellis (Baltimore), and other players with pro experience: Ed Manning (Chicago). Dorie Murray (Seattle), Stan McKenzie (Phoenix), Dale Schlueter (San Francisco). Pat Riley (San Diego), Gary Gregor (Atlanta), and Joe Kennedy (Seattle). Also, Jeff Petrie, off the Princeton campus, has a good chance of making the first five.

The Players

LEW ALCINDOR

Is Lewis Ferdinand Alcindor everything he was cracked up to be: the Big Man who would remake basketball for the Milwaukee Bucks, tailenders of the Eastern Division in 1968-69 with a 27-55 won-lost record; the terrifying shot-blocker, rebounder and scorer who would wear Bill Russell's Superman cape; the star who would bring fans and dollars galore to Milwaukee's home and away games? Well, his rookie debut is over, and the testimony is clear. He's all those things—and more.

Said Guy Rodgers, veteran NBA guard and Lew's teammate in 1969-70, "Lew is a special kind of kid, and I played with Wilt Chamberlain in the beginning and I've been in this league for a long time. Believe me, this kid is a rare human being." And in the opinion of an NBA player who faced the Alcindor challenge in court combat, the league's MVP, Willis Reed, "Nobody of his age has comparable talents. He has the ability, he has the speed and he's agile. Given time, he'll be the best center in the league." Yet another pro who's sold on Lew is hard-driving Tom Van Arsdale of the Cincinnati Royals. "I either have to throw the ball higher or pass off," Van Arsdale said, describing his frustration at trying to score against Alcindor. "He's a mountain under that basket. Nobody is going to stop him until some guy 7'10" comes along."

As for the Buck center's gifts to Milwaukee basketball, one simple description tells it all: Milwaukee won 56 games and lost just 26 last season. In other words, Lew literally turned the team around, carrying the Bucks from last place in 1969 to second in '70. And, of course, he brought in fans by the thousands and dollars by the millions—in record-breaking numbers. Small wonder, then, that he was declared the NBA's Rookie of the Year, collecting 145 of a possible 146 votes. (Someone out there clearly voted with his hate instead of his head.)

The record book tells the rest of the story of Rookie Alcindor's giant attack on the league. He scored 2,361 points in 82 games, which averaged out to 28.8 per game and placed him in runner-up position to scoring champ Jerry West. His field-goal percentage of .518 earned him seventh spot in that important department. And his 1,190 rebounds, averaging out to 14.5 a game, put him in third place in the carom competition. He even chipped in with 337 assists as part of the nearly successful Buck effort to leap from last to first.

Is Lew Alcindor the new, improved version of Bill Russell? Just a step away, according to Cincinnati coach Bob Cousy. "Alcindor is just too much," said Cousy, who played with Russell on championship Boston Celtic teams. "He's on the verge of dominating this league already, and he's just a kid."

Although it may sound that way, the new kid on the block didn't find the pros quite as easy as college competition. As a newcomer to the game where the big boys play rough, and as much for a living as for glory, Lew was swiftly initiated into the bumps-and-grinds struggle under the boards. Early in the season he came up against strong Bob Rule, the Seattle SuperSonic who has very little fat on his 6'9", 220-pound frame. Rule was pushing Alcindor around, using a lot of elbows and shoulders, apparently trying to find out how much the ex-UCLA star could take. Finally, after a flurry of sharp elbow jabs and heavy shoulder action, Alcindor exploded. What promised to be a bloody scramble was cut short by players and referees, but Big Lew was still storming after the game as he explained, "John Tresvant hit me a couple of times. Then Bob Rule stuck a finger in my eye. Man, I just went for Rule."

The word went out along the league grapevine that Alcindor was nobody's weak sister. And in case there was any doubt, Alcindor declared, "It's going to be rough for me, but I might make it just as rough for them. It works both ways, you know!"

By season's end Lew had proved he could do more than simply hold his own against everything the big kids could throw at him. He did it by total play, making his presence known at all times, whether rebounding, passing off, scoring—or matching muscle for muscle, elbow for elbow, shoulder for shoulder. And, in some ways, he found life in the National Basketball Association easier than it had been in college. He was fulfilling the predictions of John Wooden, the man who had coached 7'2" (although, it is reliably rumored that Lew towers 7'4"), 240-pound Lew through his years as center on teams that had won three successive NCAA titles for the University of California at Los Angeles. In Wooden's opinion, Lew the pro "will be the same type of player he was in college—outstanding. And he will get stronger and better each succeeding year."

Agreeing with Wooden at that time was Wes Pavalon, chairman of the board of the Milwaukee Bucks. Before the Bucks signed Lew to a long-term contract estimated to be worth $1,400,000 Pavalon was telling anyone who would listen that Alcindor was *the* basketball player the Bucks *had* to have, and *would* have, no matter what the rival American Basketball Association offered the UCLA star. And what the ABA had offered, Alcindor revealed in 1970, was a cool $3.25 million. But as far as Pavalon was concerned, the ABA would have had to "outbid the whole state of Wisconsin." It never reached that point, although Alcindor did get a fair share of the state's cash, paid by the Milwaukee franchise. The reason Lew chose the NBA was, as he explained it, he wanted each league to make one offer and he would then choose. The ABA's three-and-a-quarter-million bid obviously was not the first they made to him, and not the one he had to consider. The price Milwaukee paid was certainly repaid—and then some—as Alcindor brought *many* customers to watch him play. As Pavalon said, "It's a dream come true."

Leaping Lew was a "dream come true" a good many years before he hit the pros. He was just that in the days he played for New York's Power Memorial Academy, where he powered the high-school court team through three years of play that was blemished by just one loss. Before that loss Power had taken 71 straight games, and with Alcindor leading the way had begun another healthy string of wins that was still unbroken when Lew moved on to UCLA.

The tall, well-coordinated, intelligent youngster was also a "dream" as far as his parents were concerned. He was always a fine student and a boy who stayed out of trouble. Yet, despite the demands of schoolwork and basketball, he found time for numerous other sports—and excelled in all of them. He was particularly effective in baseball, track and swimming.

Everything seemed to come easily and naturally from the day he was born, April 16, 1947, in New York City. In fact, basketball appeared to be a good prediction for his future even then, when the 22½″ infant Lew tipped the scales at 12 pounds, 11 ounces. And he continued to grow and grow into an athletic standout, inching closer to the hoop with each year: At nine he stood 5′4″, and by the time he reached ninth grade he was a skinny 6′5″ with brains and skills to match his height.

Lew was also getting his first taste of the rough-and-tough style he would be facing through the rest of his basketball career. The opposing player's name wasn't Bob Rule when Lew's Power Memorial team played Brooklyn's Boys High School and Alcindor had an unforgettable run-in with him, but some of the action was similar. "I was leaning over this cat," Lew recalls of that long-ago game, "and all of a sudden I felt this pain in my arm. He had bit me! The kid had just been beating his head against me for the whole afternoon, and he'd lost control of his emotions, and it seemed like biting me was just the thing to do. But what a bite he had. Nice and neat and even, right down the flesh of my arm."

Competition in the college ranks didn't include any known biters, although there were plenty of bangers, shovers and scratchers who tried to stop UCLA's towering center. As a freshman at the California school, Lew led the frosh team against the varsity squad, which had won the NCAA championship the previous year. Evidently unimpressed, Lew pumped in 31 points, recorded 21 rebounds, and blocked seven shots. The varsity went down to an inglorious 75-60 defeat, and Coach Wooden's eyes gleamed at the prospect of sophomore Lew playing at pivot on the Bruins' varsity.

However, so impressed by Alcindor were the rulesmakers of college basketball, they legislated against dunking in an attempt to negate his tremendous height advantage and "keep the game possible for the little people." While nobody among the officials who passed the law would concede publicly that it was purely an anti-Alcindor weapon, all of UCLA's opponents openly referred to it as "The Alcindor Rule" and laughed at how it would hinder his point production.

Lew didn't laugh; neither did he let the rule affect his on-court actions. "I personally don't like the rule," he said, "but I don't think it's going to hurt my game. I'll still get my points. If it's aimed just at stopping me, they should know it's not going to work. Besides, I'm not the only guy who dunks."

Not only didn't it affect Alcindor's game, it brought an even stronger glow to the spotlight that continually played on his talents. His defensive artillery—shot-blocking, in particular—was something the rules-makers had overlooked. Among many teams, Southern Cal would have been happier if Lew had been legally hamstrung on defense as well as offense. In his first varsity game, playing against Southern Cal, Lew throttled USC with his complete competence. Of course, he scored well in the 105-90 rout; but he also showed he wasn't just another baskethanging "tree" with no mobility. He outhustled and outelbowed the hard-hitting USC big men to run up a total of 21 rebounds. And, in the fashion made famous by Bill Russell and now being refined by Alcindor the pro, he blocked 12 shots and thoroughly demoralized the USC squad.

Alcindor's knowledge, skill and strength improved with each successive season. Intimidating entire teams with his height and perfect timing, feeding teammates when played two-on-one and sometimes three-on-one, scoring when the opportunity was there, always rebounding—Alcindor was voted All-American (unanimously) each of his three championship years, and was twice named Player of the Year. By graduation time, Lew had a degree in History, court totals of 2,325 points and 1,367 rebounds, and a million-dollar contract. No matter how you looked at it, it was a hugely successful college career.

Perhaps the best and worst games of Alcindor's college career were played against the same team and the same man, Houston and Elvin Hayes. In the first meeting of Alcindor and Hayes, their teams were battling to win the 1967 NCAA crown. It was expected to be UCLA's hardest contest but it ended up as another easy notch on the Bruin belt. The greatest credit was given to Alcindor, who dominated Hayes in scoring, rebounding and blocked shots.

When Hayes got his chance for revenge, in the course of the 1968 season, it became an empty victory. True, Houston won, 71-69, but Alcindor was far below par, having just recovered from an eye injury that had kept him out of practice for a week before the game.

They met again in the semifinals of the '68 NCAA playoffs, and Alcindor demolished Hayes—with 19 points and 18 rebounds to 10 points and five rebounds—while UCLA crushed Houston, 101-69.

As he was in college, Alcindor continued to be a total force in the pros. Rookie of the Year, All-Star, and leader of an inspired Buck team that showed just how good it had become in the 1970 playoffs, Alcindor has indeed started a dynasty that may not be stopped unless Tom Van Arsdale's mythical 7'10" center materializes out of thin air.

WILT CHAMBERLAIN

Some call him "Wilt the Stilt," others call him "The Big Dipper," and others call him "The Temperamental Tall

Man." Still others call him names that are unprintable, names they wouldn't even think of calling him to his face, because that face can get ogre-ishly ferocious at the slightest insult, and it rises a full seven feet from the floor and tops off a massively muscular 275-pound physique. So the word around the league is, "Don't push Chamberlain too hard. If he gets angry enough, he can kill you." Which means, not only do opposing players avoid pushing Wilt *that* far, even his own coaches have hesitated to cross the line marked "Danger."

Bill van Breda Kolff came close. In the course of the 1968-69 season, van Breda Kolff and Chamberlain had disagreed a number of times as to how the game should be played. And never mind that VBK was the coach; that minor fact has never troubled the huge center when his knowledge, skill or ego was being questioned. So when they faced each other after a Laker loss to Seattle, Wilt expressed some complaints that VBK was being unfair in accusing him of not hustling. With the rest of the team looking on, the coach couldn't back down even if he wanted to, and he argued up at Chamberlain. The words got hotter, tempers matching the temperature rise, and then VBK took a threatening step toward Wilt. Fortunately, Elgin Baylor stepped between them and stopped what could have been a bloody massacre for one and the end of a basketball career for the other.

By season's end, they had matched heated words again and again, with the final result being 1) the Lakers lost the championship playoff to the Celtics, with Chamberlain riding the bench for the last five minutes of the seventh game; and 2) VBK resigned as coach, to be eventually replaced by Joe Mullaney. As a parting shot, van Breda Kolff informed his successor that "Chamberlain is uncoachable."

There is a good deal of evidence in support of VBK's declaration. Alex Hannum had to coach Wilt when they were with the 76ers, and *they* almost came to blows. Frank McGuire also failed to unlock the secret to the Wilt Chamberlain puzzle, as did Dolph Schayes before him. In fact, if you go back to Wilt's playing days at Kansas, the testimony is that coach Phog Allen also found Wilt more trouble as a person than he was worth as a player. Joe Mullaney didn't suffer the same fate last year, but then,

Chamberlain was out most of the year with a physical injury that threatened to ruin Mullaney's debut as a pro coach and the Lakers' run for the championship.

On the good and bad of Wilt, no less a person than Jerry West couldn't deliver his usually praise-filled sentences without raising a few doubts and listing some knocks. In "Mr. Clutch," written with Bill Libby, West said, "I think the key to Wilt is that he never decided how he should play. Early in his career, he may have shot too much. Now, he may not shoot enough. His style varies from game to game. Unlike Bill Russell, Wilt never settled into a groove. However, unlike Russell, Wilt bounced from team to team and his team always wanted different things of him, while Russell could remain a defensive specialist.

"With the Lakers, van Breda Kolff wanted Wilt to move around more. They even disagreed on whether he should rest Wilt from time to time. Wilt prefers to stay in, and in place, and he is used to getting his way. I think Wilt has been more versatile and a greater player than Russell, but I think Russell has been a more valuable player because he is more settled down, is better able to fit in with a team, and most important, can rise to the heights far better when it is needed.

"When Wilt joined us, we had to learn to live together off the court as well as learn to play together on the court. They say Wilt is tough to live with. He is. He has great highs and lows and no in-betweens and he is bluntly outspoken."

The most incisive thoughts behind West's appraisal is that Chamberlain, unlike Russell, contributed as much harm and dissension to the team's performance as his scoring and rebounding helped that team win games. A line-for-line appraisal of Chamberlain's 11-year record in the pros immediately suggest the teams he played for *had* to be champions. For who can match these figures: Points scored: 27,426; per-game breakdown for his full regular-season career: 34.3; rebounds: 19,233, for a per-game average of 24. The huge pivotman also holds the record for most points in one game (100), an average of over 50 points a game (50.4) for an entire season's play (1961-62), and most rebounds in one game (55). Stunning, almost unimaginable . . . and equally stunning and unimaginable is the fact that through 1969 only one team on which he played was able to go all the way to become NBA title-holders.

Then came last year. A torn tendon kept him out of action for all but 12 games of the regular-season schedule, limiting his contributions to 328 points, 221 rebounds and 49 assists. And there were all indications that he couldn't possibly get back into shape in time for the playoffs. But this is just the kind of situation to which Chamberlain responds, and he captured headlines with his determined efforts to strengthen his legs, to regain his form in daily workouts so that big No. 13 could save the day for the Lakers. And there was no denying he was needed. Without him, L.A. would never have carried the Knicks into the seventh game of the finals; without his 45 points and 27 rebounds in the sixth game of the title series, the Lakers could very well have seen another season's efforts go for nothing. But when the seventh game had ended, it was the old Wilt Chamberlain story again—another season's effort *had* gone for nothing. The Knicks blasted the Lakers from the opening moments and Chamberlain, going against a crippled Willis Reed, couldn't inspire himself or his teammates in the first half. And, playing against Nate Bowman, Reed's replacement in the second half, Chamberlain still showed none of the championship style that could have brought L.A. back into the game. One of the statistics that has plagued Chamberlain for his entire career continued to harass him in this contest: he hit on just one of 11 shots from the foul line. True, the Knicks played a brilliant brand of basketball in the deciding game, but Chamberlain is the NBA superstar with the potential to rip open a game as easily as Racquel Welch can attract a crowd just by appearing in a bikini. However, if Racquel wears a potato sack, nobody's going to give her a second look; and if Wilt doesn't use all of his tools, he's not going to impress anybody, either.

Wilt the Stilt has reached the point in his career when all he has left to boast about are records that reflect glory on himself but not on the teams he has played for. And it is no surprise that there are few people around who will defend him when it is suggested the anti-Chamberlain criticism is unfair. Bill Russell, for one, acknowledged that Wilt has immense talents, then continued, "But basketball is a team game. I go by the number of championships. I play to bring out the best in my teammates. Are you going to tell me that he brought out the best in Baylor and West?" A Laker teammate remarked in private, "When he (Chamberlain) is in the mood to play hard, and not just for himself, there's no team that can beat us. Only we never know from game to game what his mood's going to be." That kind of feeling can affect a team's attitude over a whole season, and can serve as one explanation for a superteam like the Lakers always falling short of taking the title. In '69 it was the aging Celtics, behind old-timers Bill Russell and Sam Jones, who stopped Chamberlain, West and Baylor. In '70 it was the supercharged Knicks. In 1971—if the Lakers reach the championship round— it may be the Knicks again or the Milwaukee Bucks. Whoever it is, the charts make it predictable that Chamberlain will fade in the stretch. And those same charts make it predictable that Chamberlain will have a list of reasons to show why *he* wasn't to blame. If he repeats his verbal performances of years past, he'll criticize his coach. Or he'll suggest his teammates did not take advantage of his many and varied skills. He'll point out his good games, his great games—and forget to mention the times he sulks or plays listlessly or acts contrary to what his coach thinks is best for the team.

This season promises to be an interesting one for The Dipper. It may also be a different one from those he has been used to, because Joe Mullaney showed in his freshman year as coach of the Lakers that he can handle the team. All Chamberlain proved is that he is as consistently unpredictable and unreliable as ever.

If he comes back for another try—and why shouldn't he, at $250,000 a year—the Lakers will most likely outdistance every other team in their division in regular season play. And then he'll lead them into the playoff finals—and second place again. That seems to be the fate of Wilton Norman Chamberlain . . . and any team "lucky" enough to have him at pivot.

BILLY CUNNINGHAM

Pick any of the five years Billy Cunningham has been a Philadelphia 76er, then pick just about any game in which he appeared. The same image will come to mind: Billy in non-stop action, a whirlwind of activity, a one-man gang whose shooting and rebounding, especially in the closing seconds of tight games, means the difference between winning and losing. Wherever the action is thickest, that's where he's at, on offense or defense—6'6", 220 pounds of Billy the Kid, hitting the boards and coming away with basketballs at a rate expected only of the biggest, brawniest men in the pro game.

As for acrobatic showmanship, Billy has only the past performances of Elgin Baylor as competition when it comes to driving, twisting, suspended motion, those insane, pulse-pounding attacks on the hoop in the center of heavy traffic under the backboard. It's a style of pyrotechnic play that awes teammates as much as anybody else in the league. "He hangs in the air like he's defying gravity," says fellow 76er Wally Jones. "He takes a beating and hangs in there, and that's what the game is all about. When the pressure's on, so is Billy."

"You really can't handle Billy at his best," said another teammate. "The funny thing is, I sometimes think he can't make as many of his weird shots when nobody's on him. He needs that contact, like it makes his juices really flow. And when he gets it, it's like he's playing with the neighborhood kids again, back in Brooklyn. I mean, his eyes light up. He really digs going down the middle or across it, sort of like the way Elgin Baylor used to play—hanging up there and making shots under his arms and every which way."

There isn't a man in basketball who intimidates Billy when his hand is on the ball and his eye is on the basket. When Bill Russell—the last word in defensive players— stood between Billy and the basket, Cunningham still went full-steam-ahead, and more often than not beat the old master one way or another. And when Russell retired, Big Lew Alcindor inherited the role of shot-blocker supreme. But this didn't put a halter on the Kangaroo Kid's race-horse style when Philadelphia took on the Milwaukee Bucks. The most memorable example of this came in the 1970 playoff series between the Bucks and 76ers. Not only did Billy battle Alcindor with every defensive move in the books, and a few that hadn't been written before, he consistently outmaneuvered or outfoxed the Bucks' super-rookie to ring up 50 fat points in an all-out effort that won Philly the only game it took in the five playoff contests. It was the highest number of points Billy had ever scored in pro play, and it came against the toughest defensive operator in the league.

What explanation does Billy have for his scrappy approach to the game? "When pressure situations come up," he said, "I've got to admit they offer a great challenge to me. I have to work as hard as I possibly can to get as good a shot as I can. We usually try to work some kind of play, but if that breaks down you've got to go on instinct. Are you going to try to drive and perhaps get fouled, or stop short and take a jump shot? You have to react without thinking, because you usually have only three seconds or so to make your play. You have to kind of time it yourself in your head."

About 50 percent of Billy's points are a result of his driving, forceful play, the other 50 percent coming on shots put up from behind screens established by his Philadelphia teammates. And even though his flying, diving and turning perpetual-motion moves get him into personal-foul trouble in the really bang-and-get-banged contests, it also forces the other teams' defensive men to accumulate fouls at the same rate. His wild jumping and shooting tactics often compel opponents to try to stop him body to body, which means Billy is often seen at the foul line, picking up a point here, two points there, or completing a three-point play. And late in a tight game, the enemy club finds itself in deep foul trouble. That's the kind of contribution coaches and teammates truly appreciate. "Billy fouls out a lot more than most anyone else in the league," said an NBA official, "and it doesn't look good in the year-end statistics. But to anybody who knows this game, they realize how much it costs 76er opponents in their own fouls and game plan. Billy's real value isn't reflected in the statistics—only in the team's overall record."

Cunningham's go-go game is in perfect accord with the way 76er coach Jack Ramsay likes to see basketball played. As Ramsay remarked, after Philadelphia had traded away Wilt Chamberlain in order to make the 76ers a truly fluid, free-flowing club, "I figure that, with our speed and extra defense, we can afford to give away 10 rebounds a game and still win. To do it, we must force turnovers, then handle the ball well when we get it."

That suited Billy just fine. He acknowledged that he enjoyed playing the hard and fast game Ramsay promoted, even though it meant sacrificing the mighty offensive and defensive strengths of Chamberlain. "Look," Billy said, "Chamberlain is a friend of mine. He's also a great basketball player. But with Wilt gone, everybody on our team has more to do." Everybody, or so it seemed at times, was Billy Cunningham. For not only did his scoring increase dramatically with Chamberlain gone, his rebounding totals also soared, especially when muscular Luke Jackson failed to come back from injuries to help out on the boards.

A fast look at Billy's NBA seasonal records tells the tale of his steady improvement. As a rookie, in the 1965-66 season, he averaged 14.3 points over 80 games; the next year, he advanced to an 18.5 mark in 81 games; in 1967-68, the totals read 18.9 points per game in an injury-ridden season that saw him appear in 74 contests; and for 1968-69, he could boast a 24.8 points-per-game average in 82 games, with a healthy 2,034 total points scored. However, last year he outdid himself in point production, finishing fourth in the league scoring race with 2,114 points for 81 games—an average of 26.1 per contest. And his rebounding figures are equally as impressive. From 1966, when he grabbed 599 caroms, Billy's yearly retrieve totals go this way: 589 for 1967, 562 for 1968 (in only 74 games), and a leap to 1,050 for 1969. Then, last year, he again surpassed his personal best by grabbing 1,101 rebounds in 81 tilts, earning seventh slot in the league competition in that department. In addition, he went way over his single-season high for assists—287—set in the 1968-69 season, by passing off for baskets 352 times. He also continued to play aggressive ball, picking up 331 personal fouls and being disqualified in 15 games. All of which adds up to Billy's having earned a place on the 1970 First Team All-Star squad, a repeat of the honor he received in 1969 for the first time.

In five seasons Billy has come a long way, longer and higher than he ever expected following his graduation from the University of North Carolina in 1965, where he had won recognition as an All-American forward. When Billy reported to the 76er training camp in '65, he was young, nervous and afraid. "For the first few days," he confessed, "I was sure I was going to get cut from the squad." But he stuck to the advice given him by Frank McGuire, a personal friend and the man who had acquired an enviable reputation as a coach in both the pro and collegiate ranks. "I know what it will take for you to make it," McGuire told Billy before the training camp began. "The one thing the pros will never forgive you for is not hustling. The day you show signs of not trying, you just pack your bags and go home."

Billy had no intention of going home, even though it was a good one and his parents would have welcomed him back and encouraged him as they had always done. But Billy had a wife, whom he had met at UNC, a chance to make it with the 76ers, and a pride in himself that demanded he give it everything he had. Yet he almost didn't make the team, primarily because Dolph Schayes, then the 76er coach, tried playing Billy at guard instead of his normal forward position. Cunningham's dribbling and passing were not quite up to standards for a pro backcourt man, and it looked as if his worst fears were coming true. Schayes, however, gave up on the experiment and returned Billy to forward, where everything fell into place. "After a few games," Schayes said, "I realized that Bill would never be able to take full advantage of his potential—his driving and leaping—unless we moved him back inside."

What followed was a great season that saw Billy edged out by the fabulous shooting Rick Barry for Rookie-of-the-Year honors. But Cunningham got Dolph Schayes' award as the best, and these words from his coach: "He did all the things I like to see in a ballplayer," Schayes said after the season. "If he was played tough, he'd free himself instead of letting up. Billy's a schoolyard player. He's loose. He can give-and-go as long as you ask him. He does everything a rookie must do to make it big. First, he thinks under pressure. Second, he's a great competitor who loves to battle for the rebounds. Finally, he goes all-out, with or without pain, as evidenced by his play late in the season even though he was bothered by a bad back for almost a month."

A New Yorker himself, Schayes was well acquainted with the "backboard jungle" roughhouse basketball Brooklyn kids cut their teeth on, as well as break those teeth along with an occasional arm or leg. And Billy confirmed it by saying, "Much of my jumping ability came from those rough-and-tumble beginnings. Basketball in the playgrounds is war, and the New York guys have a style of their own. They're tremendous ball-handlers and they are guys hard enough to jump out of buildings. In Philadelphia I've found that the kids can shoot better. But the New York guys drive a lot more, because they have to fight for the ball. So we learned to drive a lot, and fight for possession."

Which helps to account for why, from his rookie season on, Billy entrenched himself as a fighting, slam-bang, scoring kind of player the Philadelphia fans loved. Management shared their enthusiasm, in words and salary, and Billy seemed a permanent fixture in Philly. Thus it came as a bombshell when he announced, in 1969, that he had signed a contract to play for the Carolina Cougars of the American Basketball Association in two years. Would he be playing for Carolina in 1970-71, he was asked, or would he sit out the year because of certain unresolved legal points and contract definitions? "Nothing has been decided yet," Billy answered. "I do know that eventually I want to play with the Cougars. I have a contract with them and my wife and I have been looking for a home in North Carolina. We like it down there."

With the ABA still a step behind the NBA in development of top teams and players, Billy could really tear the league apart. But wherever he plays, the fans will get their money's worth in action, thrills and a view of basketball at its best. For when Billy Cunningham is in motion with that round ball, it's the game that counts, not where it's played. And the game, in Billy's terms, is spelled H-U-S-T-L-E!

DAVE DeBUSSCHERE

On paper, the Knicks are a small team, one that doesn't seem prepared to stay on an even par with the tall-men clubs over the course of an 82-game schedule. Willis Reed—anywhere between 6-8 and 6-10, depending on which authority you believe—is the tallest man on the club, so the New Yorkers have to give away several inches to opponents in a game where inches matter very much. And at one of the forward positions the Knicks play Dave DeBusschere, 6-6 and 220 pounds, asking him to match moves and muscle with men usually 6-8 or more. Yet Dave, like the rest of the team, doesn't merely equal the men he faces in each game's mismatch, he outplays them. As he did in last season's playoffs, when every game was critical, when pressures mounted to points of explosion, when injuries threatened to destroy a dream the Knicks had been building win by win over a wearying schedule. But through it all DeBusschere's strength and stamina grew, not once did he let up. Not against Baltimore's Bullets, who played inspired ball in an attempt to reverse the New York domination over them since the 1968-69 playoffs—DeBusschere battled Gus Johnson with a fury that added fuel to the fire of Knick fans who felt Dave, not Gus, rated a First Team designation when the votes were tallied for the All-NBA team. Not against the Milwaukee Bucks, with Lew Alcindor trying to be a one-man gang—DeBusschere not only played his man at forward, he collapsed on Big Lew in a successful effort to lift the load off Willis Reed's shoulders. Not against the Los Angeles Lakers, on paper a power that could very well have swamped the smaller Knicks—DeBusschere handled the great Elgin Baylor and still was able to move over to tangle with huge Wilt Chamberlain, an even more impressive threat than ever with Reed virtually incapacitated by injury. Playing Chamberlain, Dave looked, as one sportswriter phrased it, "like a tourist leaning on the Empire State Building."

Attitude is a word that applies to how the Knicks did what they had to do to win it all last year. And thinking of himself as part of a team that functions well only when all of its parts are working perfectly, Dave said, "What I like about the Knicks is that there is no superstar, so to speak, who must get points to help us. We're well-balanced. We're believing in ourselves as a team. There isn't a night we have stepped on the floor since I've been with the club that we didn't think we'd win . . . and win big."

This is the attitude the Knicks acquired when they traded Walt Bellamy and Howard Komives to Detroit for DeBusschere two seasons ago. In Bellamy they had the big center who, they hoped, would make them a contender. But Bellamy was inconsistent, the equal of Wilt Chamberlain some nights, the opposite on other nights. And to play their kind of game, the Knicks needed consistency on defense, offense—all aspects of play. They got it when Bellamy left and DeBusschere arrived. After Dave had been with the team a couple of weeks, Willis Reed, delighted to be back at center now that DeBusschere was in his corner slot, said, "To me, Dave is a tough veteran forward who knows the game. He gives 100 percent effort every night. He's an unselfish player. The only thing he's interested in is winning. I'm glad that I don't have to play against him anymore—he was the guy I'd pair against when we played the Pistons."

Author Jonathan Baumbach evaluated the new Knicks this way: "If statistics could be trusted, Bellamy had a better season than DeBusschere (in 1968-69): he averaged 17.4 points a game to DeBusschere's 16.3, took 1,101 rebounds to DeBusschere's 888. To account for DeBusschere's accomplishment you had to see him play. He and Reed were more effective in tandem off the boards for their first game together than Bellamy and Reed at their most congenial. For his height . . . DeBusschere is as good a rebounder as any man in the league with the possible exceptions of Lucas and Unseld. He is a fine outside shot, handles the ball with the adeptness of a smaller man, and is exceptionally tough on defense. During his early games, DeBusschere, concentrating on rebounding and defense—his role on the team—seemed to fit in as if he had been playing with the Knicks for years. Roundly built, almost soft-looking from a distance, he plays with inconspicuous grace—his style not to be stylish.

"It seemed to the Knick fan that New York acquired with DeBusschere the kind of balance and esprit of the best Boston teams, though with a style of their own."

That "style" can best be described in one word: defense. Last season's championship drive was based on the fact that New York allowed their opponents fewer points per game (105.9), than any other NBA team. So it was fitting that three of the five players named to the league's All-Defensive Team, first five, should be Knicks—Frazier, Reed and DeBusschere. It was the second year that the NBA had selected an All-Defensive Team, and Frazier and DeBusschere were the only two repeaters from the 1968-69 first five.

Dave has been on somebody's all-something team since his early athletic beginnings in Detroit, Michigan. And back in his teen years baseball played as important a part in his gamesmanship as did basketball. When he was 17, DeBusschere pitched a local sandlot team to a national junior championship. Two years later he did it again from the mound, hurling another Detroit team to a national senior championship. Playing both baseball and basketball at Austin High School, he made All-City in both sports, pitching the baseball team to a city Catholic championship and powering the court squad to a state championship.

He could count on making a professional living in either sport, or both, and this thought played a large part in his decision regarding college. By the time he graduated from Austin High, 18-year-old Dave had 40 basketball scholarship offers to choose from, some inviting him to play for top national teams. But the University of Detroit had strong varsity teams in baseball and basketball, was close to home, and he made the U of D his selection. Four years later he had a degree in marketing and a national reputation as a top athlete in both sports.

In three years of varsity baseball Dave pitched the team into three NCAA regional tournaments. In those same three years he also propelled the Titans into two NIT tournaments and one NCAA tournament, averaging 24.8 points per game over those three varsity seasons. After a showing like that, the pro offers started rolling in. On the baseball side, the White Sox bait of a $70,000 contract was the one that tempted him the most. And the following season he posted a 10 won, 1 lost record pitching for the Sox's Savannah farm club. His won-lost mark and 2.49 Earned Run Average won him a late-season shot on the major-league roster, and he looked good in his few appearances.

He was also drafted by the Detroit Pistons in 1962, and that season he signed a $15,000 contract, then earned it by averaging 12.7 ppg in regular-season play and a 20 ppg average in the playoffs. The following season Dave the pitcher was limited by a sore arm, and Dave the cage star was able to see action in only 15 Piston games because of a broken leg. But his basketball fortunes rose in 1964-65, when he made the solid contributions of an all-round player with a 16.7 ppg average and 874 rebounds, plus playing strong defense at one end of the court and passing off for 253 baskets.

In 1964 and '65 the White Sox couldn't make room for him on their pitching-rich roster, so he continued throwing for their Triple-A club. But his disappointment at not making the parent club was getting deeper, and when Piston owner Fred Zollner asked him to give up baseball—and sweetened the request with additional dollars—Dave reversed his statement of the previous year, "Baseball and basketball—they're like breakfast and supper. When you get up you like one, and later on you like the other. But at the time, each tastes as good as the other. As for my sports, it depends on the time of the year." After Zollner's offer, Dave said, "The area of my responsibility has grown too large for me to try to pursue dual careers." So much for the White Sox.

Part of the responsibility to which he referred was his new role as player-coach of the Pistons, a weighty burden for a 24-year-old. He did the best he could until 1967, when he relinquished the coaching position, saying, "I never asked for the job. I never campaigned for it. They came to me. Our team was disrupted, in a state of chaos. I knew I was too young to coach. But what else could I do? I wanted to see things get straightened out."

In those pre-Knick seasons, Dave's steady scoring was reflected in his yearly averages: 16.7 in 1965; 16.4 in '66; 18.2 in '67; and 17.9 in '68. His rebounds kept the same pace, with a high of 1,081 in the 1967-68 season. Nothing changed in 1968-69, most of which he spent on the Knick roster, as he finished the schedule with 888 rebounds and a 16.3 ppg average. Nothing changed, that is, except he was now with a team that had the potential of wearing the NBA crown. Aware of this, Dave's first response to the trade was, "It's like being reborn," followed by, "I'll do my best to make New York a winner."

That he did last year, playing his hard-nosed defensive game, clicking with the Knick slickness in ball- and team-control, posting final figures of 790 rebounds, 194 assists, and a scoring average of 14.6 points a game.

Dave will be 30 this year but there is no indication that time has made any inroads on his strength, energy or skills. He's still the same guy Willis Reed described as a 100-percent player, an unselfish team man. The same guy who comes into each game thinking, "There isn't a night we have stepped on the floor . . . that we didn't think we'd win." With that kind of guy, it's pretty hard to lose.

WALT FRAZIER

The quarterback of the Knicks is a testimony to 1) what a man can do to develop his talents to their highest degree of use; 2) what a coach means to each player and the whole team; and 3) how important defensive play is in the league where anybody can break up a ball game. On Point One: Walt Frazier has the quickest hands of any player in the NBA and the cat-quick moves to get those hands into position to flick out and steal the ball. But, along with these natural attributes, he developed a psychological attack on opponents that make his physical weapons doubly dangerous. "I wait for a guy to get careless," Frazier said, "like on the pass-in, when a guy is mad because his man has just scored. Then, if I steal off him, he'll tend to tighten up and then you can really put the pressure on him." (Exhibit A of how successfully this works is the collapse of the Lakers in last season's playoff series against the Knicks.) Then, Frazier continued, "If the guy I'm guarding is a good outside shooter, I try to force him to drive on me rather than let him set up for a shot. If he is a good layup man, then I try to make him take the outside shot. I also feel a concentrated stare into his eyes is better than my doing a lot of jumping around." On Point Two: In 1968, Walt wasn't playing up to his potential and he was letting it get to him. Enter Red Holzman, coach of the Knickerbockers. Holzman told Frazier that he was dribbling too much and slowing down the tempo of the team's offense. Said Frazier, "Red told me that if I was going to do all that dribbling, I should at least head for the basket. Try to penetrate. It's a simple thing when you think about it, but it took Red to spot it and make me aware of it." And then, when Frazier was "wondering if I could really make it in this league," Holzman took him aside and said, "I know you're better than you're showing out there, because I scouted you in college myself." And, as Frazier concluded, "We had a man-to-man talk, and it gave me the shot of confidence that I needed." On Point Three: "Walt," said Dave De-Busschere, "could strip a car with the engine running." Which is to say that Walt can hound an opponent into the ground, break up the impetus of an enemy team on the upswing, distract and finally destroy the coordination of five men wearing the "wrong" uniform on court. He takes the best of them—Monroe, West, Bing, Robertson—and forces them into mistakes, fraction-of-a-second hesitations that make all the differences in a game built on split-second moves and decisions.

What Frazier accomplished in the course of the 1969-70 season made him one of the top contenders for the MVP prize which eventually went to teammate Reed. But Walt didn't come away empty-handed. He was the leading vote-getter on the NBA's list of All-Defensive players, a repeat of his 1968-69 showing in this balloting. Walt also played his usual outstanding game as a starting guard for the East in the All-Star game. And he was selected as a member of the First Team NBA All-Star squad.

His statistics for the season past demonstrate as clearly as anything just how steadily he has improved. Walt's 1,609 points scored in 77 games came to a per-contest average of 20.9. Compared to his rookie figures of 666 points and a 9.0 ppg mark, and his sophomore totals of 1,403 points and a 17.5 ppg mark, his 1970 record clearly exhibits his rise as a scoring power. His 629 assists, good for an 8.2 per-game average, placed him second only to Lenny Wilkens in that department. And if his steals were somehow worked into the assists column . . .

At 6-4, 202 pounds, Frazier looks similar to the young ballplayer who joined the Knicks off the campus of Southern Illinois University. As a Saluki under the tutelage of coach Jack Hartman, Walt learned the importance of defense. "Most guys play defense straight up," Frazier said, "but with Hartman you learned to play in a crouch. He drilled us on this all the time. It was a reaction drill: Left, right, back. We did it so much you couldn't straighten up. But if you didn't play defense for Hartman, you didn't play."

The way it paid off for Frazier as a freshman Knick was summarized by Willis Reed. "When Walt came to his first training camp with us," Reed said, "we could see immediately that he was the best young guard on the squad at the time. Not quite like Barnett, who is a different-style player . . . and remember, I'm talking about a guy coming up. Walt moved the club very well up and down the court. He looked sharp handling the ball and he looked very good on defense."

Frazier looked very good on the football field as well as the basketball court when he was playing high-school sports. In Atlanta, Ga., where he was a high-school superhero, Walt was even better known for his handling of a football than a basketball. He recognized that athletics hadn't reached the point of finding a spot in pro football for a black quarterback, so instead of hoping the gridiron world would grow up in a hurry, he shifted his emphasis to the indoor sport with the round ball. And when football scholarship offers began arriving from schools such as Indiana and Kansas, he turned them down; in fact, he decided against those same two schools when they extended basketball scholarships. He opted, instead, for relatively unknown Southern Illinois University, in Carbondale, Illinois. Among the feats he accomplished for Jack Hartman's Salukis was leading them to a 24-2 record in his last year, which earned them a bid to the National Invittation Tournament. That NIT ended with Walt's team the champion and Frazier himself the Most Valuable Player.

The more Frazier played in the pros, the more confident he grew. He eventually reached the point where he totally believed in his dribbling ability, which meant much behind-the-back ball-moving. It looks flashy and showboat until you realize that Walt has the ball under perfect control, and that this style keeps it away from harassing defenders.

After watching Frazier develop in three years to what he is now, writer Dave Sendler wrote this evaluation: "Perhaps Walt's most exciting way to beat teams is his defense," although his offensive play was always reliably there whenever the Knick scoring needed a pickup. "He had become so proficient at stealing the ball and disrupting the opponents' offensive patterns that teams began to devise special measures to control his marauding. The Detroit Pistons instructed guard Howard Komives, who usually plays Frazier head-to-head, to move away from the ball and the rest of the Pistons when Detroit was on the attack. The plan was to keep Frazier away from the flow of the game. Los Angeles and some of the other teams tried the same strategy. At times it helped, but the Knicks countered by putting Frazier on the other team's most valuable man with the ball. The Knicks were thus challenging rivals to sacrifice their best backcourt players just to get Frazier away from the action. Usually, the teams were unwilling to do this. Thus Frazier still had ample opportunity to upset the best-laid plans of New York's opponents."

Nineteen-seventy was a season dedicated, it seems, to Frazier upsetting any plans devised by Knick opponents to upset the Knicks. And Knick fans—those sophisticated New Yorkers who watch, play and criticize basketball as their way of life—came pouring through the turnstiles of Madison Square Garden not to chew the Knicks to pieces but to cheer them to the rafters. Frazier got more than his share of their love, devotion and raves. When they set up their cry of "Deee-fense!" Frazier, more than any other Knick, was their man. When they looked for the threadneedle pass, Frazier, even more than Bradley and Barnett, was the sharp-eyed one to make them happy. (In the last game of the playoffs, Walt passed off for 19 assists, tying Bob Cousy's playoff record.) When things got tight and a sudden burst of baskets was the Knick need, Clyde Frazier (so-called for his Twenties style of dress) fed off to the cutting man or carried the mail himself. They feed Frazier, those Knick-krazy fans, and Walt feeds them right back in as emotional a give-and-take as has ever been enjoyed by players and fans anywhere, anytime. "I don't worry about a thing," Frazier said during the 1970 season. "I never get excited, I just go along, real passive. The only time I get woke up is at the end when I sense it, the crowd and the noise, and I see all the guys running all over the place."

Knick broadcaster Marv Albert couldn't find enough words to extoll Frazier's play by the time the Knicks had run up a record string of 18 straight wins. But Albert wasn't alone among broadcasters. Wherever the New York team played, broadcasters were echoing the sentiments of former coach and referee Charlie Eckman, who heaped glory on Frazier following a New York victory over the Baltimore Bullets, for whom Eckman is home broadcaster. "You might have seen the best guard in the league tonight," he told his television audience. "What did Frazier do? What didn't he do? He passed, he saw, he shot, he stole the ball, he played defense and he refereed. He did everything but serve lunch. He's the best guard I've seen since Oscar."

That kind of comparison would have pleased Frazier a year or two ago. Not now. Now Frazier is himself, one of a kind. He's not Oscar Robertson because his style is geared to mesh with four other men on the floor. He's not Oscar because he'll as quickly pass off to the free man for a shot, even when he's in position to take the two pointer. He's not Oscar Robertson because he's seen his kind of play pay off in a world championship. As Frazier said during the Knick surge to the title, "Everybody wants his own identity, and I want mine!"

His identity is secure because nobody who has ever played the backcourt put it all together quite the way Clyde does. He's back again this year with his bag of tricks intact, and it's hard to imagine what more he can do to surpass last year's display of all-court mastery. But knowing Clyde, he'll come up with that something new to keep Knick opponents a half-step behind their flying pace—and several points behind at the end of the game.

JOHN HAVLICEK

Most athletes consider the game they play as a business, an activity that is, in many ways, the same as a 9-to-5 job, only with different hours and different demands. That's usually your run-of-the-mill athlete, the one who fills out the lineup, sticks around (if he's lucky) until he's earned his pension, and disappears. The star, though, is something else. He gets to work long before the other guys, stays long after they've left, and pours everything he has into his hours on the job. In the game of professional basketball, that's a John Havlicek.

"John is fast, but there are faster players," said Tom Meschery of the Seattle SuperSonics. "So John doesn't outspeed anyone, he outconditions everyone. Late in a game, when everyone's tired, there'll be a loose ball. John and another guy will go for the ball. The other guy reaches down within himself for an extra burst of energy, and so does John, but John comes up with just that little bit more."

Game after game, season after season, Havlicek finds that "little bit more." And he becomes what former Boston Celtic teammate Larry Siegfried described as "the complete player. John hustles, he plays both ends of the court, he runs, he shoots. He is like a living tradition."

And so, going into the 1969-70 season, Havlicek—the living tradition of the champion Celtics, a passing tradition—knew he had to dig down and come up with more than just a little bit more. For Bill Russell and Sam Jones had really retired and the burden of play, of scoring, of rebounding came to rest even more on John's muscular shoulders. Without Russell there to get the ball and Jones to gun 'em down in the clutch, the Boston five couldn't match the strengthened Knicks, Bullets, Bucks and 76ers. For the first time in the memory of man, the Celtics failed to make the playoffs—but it wasn't the fault of John Havlicek. Called upon to be a one-man gang, he came through with his finest season ever. At the conclusion of the 1970 schedule, John had placed eighth in the NBA scoring race, pumping in 1,960 points at an average of 24.2 per game, a huge leap over his previous career highs for a season of 1,771 points and a 21.6 average in 1968-69. And last year, because he *had* to, John put in 3,369 minutes of floor time in 81 games. It was the most playing time the 30-year-old Celtic had logged, his previous high having been 3,174 minutes in 82 games. John also ended up tying Walt Hazzard for sixth place among the league's assists leaders, with an average of 6.8 per game—another personal career mark. And not only did his 635 rebounds exceed the retrieving efforts of any other Celtic, it bypassed his own personal best of 570, racked up in 1969.

The more they ask of him, the more he gives. Yet what makes Havlicek the star he is? What drives him to be more than any other player, to be more than his own potential would indicate? The word that is repeated around the league is "pride." Pride in being the best, doing his best, in knowing that he didn't fail his teammates and himself. It is part of what sports experts call "the will to win," that intangible quality that helps sideline observers to understand the inner force dictating Havlicek's dogged defense, steady scoring and inexhaustible drive. Also, it is the realistic approach to life that says to Havlicek, "Not only does the reward come in titles and trophies, it also comes in dollars."

John combined these two elements—pride and money— when, before a crucial playoff game with the Philadelphia 76ers, during the 1965-66 eliminations, he wrote on the locker room blackboard: "$80,000," then told his teammates, "That's how much we win if we go all the way to the finals." After that comment, he chalked the word, "Pride," on the slate. Taking this compelling attitude into the game, Boston defeated the 76ers, after which Havlicek told a friend, "Pride is the thing that can push you to get the money." It was the same pride that took John and the Celtics all the way to the 1968-69 championship, defeating the Los Angeles Lakers and earning top money of $93,-000. And it was the same pride that made him the running, scoring, rebounding tornado he was in 1969-70, even though Boston was obviously not the contender it had been for so many years.

When talking of the glory of the Celtics, and of Havlicek's share in that remarkable tradition, Boston fans invariably refer to the sixth game of the 1968-69 Eastern Division playoff finals. It was a hard-fought series between the Celtics and the Knicks. Boston had been enjoying an easy contest until the Knicks suddenly erupted for a slew of points and were threatening to overtake the Celtics in the closing minutes of play. New York baskets kept on cutting the margin to a thin two-point edge time and again, only to have one man—John Havlicek—stop them from knotting the score as he repeatedly raised the Boston lead to four points. And each bucket he hit was scored with time running out on the 24-second clock. The one that made it 103-99, Celtics, caused Bill Russell to rave, "It was a crazy, wild shot—an unbelievable shot." The one that upped the Boston lead to 105-101 and sewed up the game was a fantastic show of confidence and skill that only a cool, self-assured veteran could have pulled off—or even considered.

Boston was moving the ball around, keeping it away from the Knicks as the clock flashed away the valuable seconds. Then Havlicek got the ball with under 10 seconds left for Boston to take a shot. He protected the ball, then faked left, faked right, faked a third time, then began to dribble. With every Boston fan yelling, "Shoot!" Havlicek checked the clock and saw there were just five seconds left. But instead of gunning for the hoop, he ate up three more seconds in a drive to the baseline before letting go an off-balance, almost impossible shot. The nets rippled and the Celtic margin was back up to four points. "Baby, I can't believe it," marveled Larry Siegfried. And with those two heartstopping baskets, John Havlicek had shattered the Knick dream of a comeback victory and a shot at dethroning the Celtics in a seventh, winner-take-all contest.

In the locker room after the game, Havlicek retained the same cool attitude he had exhibited on court. Of those key baskets he said, "Well, the first one was kind of a prayer shot. I just wanted to get it up near the rim. The clock was running out and I figured we'd get a chance for the rebound, even if the shot didn't go in." Several reporters shook their heads, as if to suggest that John was being modest, but he just laughed aside their gestures and went on to describe the second last-second shot. "Now, on that last one I could have taken the 15-footer, only when I looked at the clock I saw there were five seconds left. That's an awful long time in that situation. So I used up a little more time . . . then shot."

Bill Russell, Boston's coach and center, had a lot more to say about Havlicek's exciting play, and in far more excited words. "That first one was fantastic, too much," Russell repeated to anyone who would listen. "But the second one . . . that second one . . ." Russell's hands displayed the disbelief he simply couldn't express in mere words.

Writers, fans and teammates have often been witness to Havlicek heroics which have left them groping for the right words to express the wonder and admiration he inspires. For no matter which sport he is playing, he gives it everything he has—and that's a lot. As he told one reporter, "The day I play a game and it doesn't matter whether I win or lose, that's the day I retire."

Retirement is still something for future consideration for the NBA hustler who was born April 8, 1940, in little Martin's Ferry, Ohio. A lover of action and activity, John spent his pre-teen years hunting and fishing, involved in the outdoor life and developing a body that became a perfect mechanism for anything connected with athletics. Growing up in Lansing, Ohio, he excelled in every sport he tried—basketball, football, baseball, track, tennis, swimming. . . . On the baseball field, competing against players that included several who would become big-leaguers, he starred at every infield position and batted between .400 and .500 each year. He was just as extraordinary as the quarterback of a football team that played in a very tough league, and his high-school gridiron efforts won him all-state honors. But he rejected Woody Hayes's invitation to play football at Ohio State University because he wanted time to study, something else at which John got high marks, as proven by his B average at OSU.

There was time for basketball, though. And playing on

OSU teams that boasted such scorers as Jerry Lucas and Larry Siegfried, John naturally developed his talents as a defensive whiz. So good was he that he was on permanent assignment to handle the opponents' toughest players while Ohio's shooters were putting in the points. Nevertheless, Havlicek recorded a fair number of baskets and, in his junior and senior years, showed a shooting percentage of better than 50 percent. Then he joined the Celtics in 1962 and looked around to see a team loaded with great shooters, which led him to decide he'd be able to do more for the team by playing sharp defense and feeding off. He was doing an excellent job of it, too—until Coach Arnold "Red" Auerbach told him, "The other teams know you're not going to shoot when you get the ball. That's not helping us any. Take your shot." And, as Havlicek says, "I've been shooting 'em up ever since."

Famed as "the best sixth man" ever to play pro ball, Havlicek was described by writer John Devaney this way: "In game after game he physically beats some of the best-conditioned athletes in the world—the guards and forwards of the National Basketball Association. He beats them by running and running . . . and running some more, and they marvel how he beats them, and they wish, Lord how they wish, they could run the way he runs."

Playing more in 1969-70 than he'd ever played before, and as a starter rather than as a sixth man, John ran more than ever—and was better than ever. He may be a member of the over-30 club, but time doesn't seem to have made a dent in the Running Machine. The 1970-71 season promises to be more of the same for John Havlicek: running, scoring, putting a flame under the rest of the squad and keeping it burning from start to finish. And if Boston can come up with a center to add what's been missing since the retirement of Bill Russell, Havlicek just might run the Celtics right back up to the top of the flagpole.

CONNIE HAWKINS

"Of all the poor people I knew in New York, Connie was the poorest." The man who made this observation was Billy Cunningham, another basketball superstar born in Brooklyn and raised on a daily diet of concrete courts and hard-hitting play. Today, neither Cunningham nor Hawkins can be considered anywhere near poor; indeed, Hawkins is right up there with the wealthiest athletes in any sport. He's a million-dollar ballplayer now, but it didn't look as though he'd be anything but a hardship case for life until Fortune finally tuned in to his troubles . . .

Connie was born on July 17, 1940, in a Brooklyn slum. One of six children, by the time he was ten years old his father had disappeared and his mother was almost totally blind. But instead of giving in to the temptations surrounding him—to steal, run with a gang, make the dope scene—he let off his frustrations and anger on schoolyard basketball courts. And he also attended classes with regularity at Boys High School, although the diploma he received at graduation didn't explain that he could barely read the words that declared him eligible for an even higher education.

What he did earn at the Brooklyn high school was applause for the tremendous performances he put on as star of the varsity basketball team. The applause was loudest at Madison Square Garden, when 18,000 fans roared him on to greater and greater efforts as he led Boys High to two city championships. But he outdid his best previous efforts as a member of the East squad in the 1960 high school seniors' All-Star game. Playing against him for the West team were several future professional stars—Jeff Mullins, Joe Caldwell, George Wilson, Paul Silas—but nobody was good enough to stop him that day.

The game was played on an outdoor court that was slick and dangerously dotted with small pools of water. Rain and fog threatened to ruin the day for fans and players alike. And it was a dull game as the players moved cautiously over the court, ball squirting out of wet hands, sneakers squishing to sliding stops in the puddles. It went that way for three quarters and then, in the words of a reporter who covered the contest, "an East player began to perform miracles, began to move over the treacherous surface like some scuba diver through water. Where others had merely walked on the wet wood, a graceful, long-armed 6'7" youngster began to run on it—then fly. And, all of a sudden, the game was no longer competition. He was grabbing the rebounds, as he had been doing all along, only now he was no longer pitching out to his guard to set the fast break in motion. Now he was scrubbing the boards clean and dribbling the length of the floor himself, leading the fast break and capping it off with dunk shots or Cousy-like behind-the-back passes to teammates as he floated toward the basket, drawing the defense with him.

"On a dry court, the sight of a big man rebounding, leading the fast break and capping it off with fancy assists would boggle the imagination, but on a wet court it defied belief. Yet time and again it was happening. The final score was East 85, West 60, and a tremendous individual victory for one young man. The man, the winner of the Most Valuable Player trophy in this game, was Connie Hawkins."

That kind of player, even though his education would have won him no trophies, is highly attractive to fame-and-glory-oriented colleges throughout the United States. So it was no cause for surprise that nearly 250 institutions of higher education extended scholarship offers to Connie. (Have you ever looked up the word "scholarship" in the dictionary?) The one made by the University of Iowa sounded just right to young Hawkins, and his college career began.

And ended—in a hurry—amid the uproar caused by a scandal that smeared the good name of basketball, a sport that has more than once had its good name in jeopardy. The trouble had begun for Hawkins during high school, when a one-time basketball star named Jack Molinas befriended the Brooklyn youngster. Molinas kept on turning up wherever Connie was playing, whether in varsity games or on the playgrounds of Brooklyn, the latter being the scene of many classic encounters featuring top high-school players as well as fine college competitors and even some pros. After the game Molinas would treat Hawkins and another New York City star, Roger Brown (now in the ABA), to dinner. Hawkins also borrowed $200 from Molinas on one occasion, and quickly repaid it.

Those dinners and that short-term loan proved more costly than Hawkins could ever have imagined. For, in April of 1961, Iowa freshman Hawkins was picked up by men from the office of New York District Attorney Frank Hogan and taken back to a New York hotel. There the 21-year-old was questioned for hours on end, until Hogan's men had collected evidence to "prove" that Molinas and a cohort had bribed players to fix games for them. Although Hawkins admitted to having taken money, there was no other evidence against him. And his admission of that came after long, confusing hours of questioning. Nevertheless, when Molinas was convicted and sent to jail, Connie was unofficially convicted by association with the gambling set. As a result, Iowa cancelled his scholarship and no other school would touch him. The last, and most crushing, blow of all was the report that the NBA, seeking to keep its reputation clear of any association with gambling, had declared Connie permanently untouchable.

Hawkins drifted aimlessly for a year, until the American Basketball League was formed and he was invited to play with the Pittsburgh Rens for $6,500. He grabbed the offer, glad to be back in action, and won the league's MVP award after a season against some pretty strong competition. Feeling secure at last, he married and moved his bride to Pittsburgh. His new-found security vanished midway into the next season when the league folded.

Help came again, this time in the form of the Harlem Globetrotters and a salary of $125 a week. "In my four years with the Globetrotters," Connie said later, "I picked up a lot of knowledge and experience. Sweetwater Clifton, the ex-Knickerbocker, taught me a lot about ballhandling. I also went against a lot of stars like Wilt Chamberlain and Oscar Robertson. Of course, I only played guys like that on playgrounds and such, but I always felt I could hold my own with them." Chamberlain, Robertson, and many other ace basketball players agreed with Hawkins, emphasizing that he belonged in the NBA, where his skills would be used to great advantage and benefit the league in general.

But nothing like that happened, and it wasn't until 1967 that Connie's life got another lift. At this point he was no longer with the Globetrotters, he had a wife and two children—and very little income. "I was worried," he said. "I was 26 and playing this game was all I could really do. Sure, I had a family to support, but my mind was infected with basketball. Always has been. I couldn't get interested in doing anything else." The solution to his problems came in the form of the American Basketball Association; 1967 was its first year and he was signed to play by the Pittsburgh Pipers.

In repayment for his first year's salary of $15,000, Connie averaged 26.8 points a game, pulled down 945 rebounds as a 6'8", 215-pound center, led the Pipers to the league title—"When we won I cried."—and took home the ABA's Most Valuable Player award. The following year, despite being hampered by injuries and the flu, Connie earned All-ABA status again with a 30.2 scoring pace and with a rebound average that placed him fifth in the league's carom race.

The jackpot at the end of Connie's rainbow finally turned up before the 1968-69 season got underway. The National Basketball Association decided they were, after all, interested in Hawkins. Contributing to this decision in no small way was the suit against the NBA being brought on Connie's behalf by a Pittsburgh lawyer named David Litman. The league's officials allowed as how they would be pleased to give "The Hawk" a contract to play with one of their teams if he would drop the $6-million case. As the NBA's board of governors put it, in part: "We simply had an indefensible stand. We had wronged this boy, if not by being party to the original act, by supporting it later. We wanted to right a wrong."

The right was wronged and, after a coin-flip to determine which would be the lucky team, Connie was signed to a very healthy contract by the Phoenix Suns. What it amounted to was $100,000 a year for three years, and other financial benefits which would eventually total more than a million dollars. All this mattered greatly to Connie, although the cash couldn't possibly erase from his memory bank the mental and physical pain he had known for so many years. However, it did restore lost dignity, allow him to enjoy many luxuries previously denied him—and it gave him the long-awaited chance to play against the best in basketball.

One of the first lessons he learned is that NBA play demands as much defensive ability as offensive. Whereas a player can be somewhat less of a defensive player in the ABA, if he can score well, the NBA expects its men to be complete players, or certainly at least competent on defense. That Connie had never been expected to play strong defense soon showed in his first game under Johnny Kerr, his coach at the beginning of the season. But, as the schedule progressed, he showed flashes of improvement. No less an authority than Red Holzman, coach of the New York Knickerbockers and a stickler for defensive basketball, said of Connie, "Hawkins is a complete player. You have to like him, because he plays both ends of the floor. I'd hate to see him get any better—he's too good now."

Soon Johnny Kerr was praising Connie regularly before resigning as coach in the middle of the 1969-70 season. "Connie helps us in so many ways," Kerr said. "He's a great passer, a fine shooter inside and outside, and a terrific rebounder on both boards. He's more agile than any big man who ever played this game and as quick as most little men. The tricks he picked up with the Globetrotters make him a real crowd-pleaser, like Cousy, Baylor and Earl Monroe."

Kerr's sentiments were soon being echoed by Jerry Colangelo, the Suns' general manager who took over the coaching job from Kerr. "Connie really took charge of some games," he said, "like I've been waiting to see all year. He won some all by himself. You have to remember, he had to go through a period of adjustment. He had his problems adjusting to the officials and the way they called things. They call more offensive fouls in the NBA than in the ABA and he found that tough to cope with."

Connie himself wasn't sure how his first year would turn out. Before the season began, he had told a reporter, "The big thing is, I got my chance now. I never went to jail, but was sentenced to eight years in some kind of prison, waiting for a chance to prove myself. It was like dying of thirst with a faucet running in front of you and your hands tied behind your back. Now I've been cut free. I can reach out for what I want. I want to prove myself. Not to the NBA. Not to the press. Not to anyone but me. I got to prove me to me."

, The proof of how Connie fared in his belated entrance into the NBA can be found in the records. The fact that Phoenix moved from a last-place finish in 1969 to a fourth-place finish in 1970 says a lot for Connie's presence in the lineup. And his statistics explain in numbers what he added to the Suns' punch. His 1,995 points and 24.6 average for 81 games earned him sixth position in the NBA scoring derby. In addition, he grabbed 846 rebounds and picked up 391 assists. So it came to pass that the 30-year-old newcomer was voted a place on the league's All-Star Second Team.

Now, with a full year of NBA experience behind him, Connie can be expected to do even more in 1971. And that's saying no more than should be expected of a basketball player who's been a superstar since he first started wowing 'em in the schoolyards of New York.

ELVIN HAYES

It was Elvin Hayes's first year as a pro. He was a rookie with a load of press clippings that labeled him superstar, and a contract for lots of dollars that made him the envy of many already established and talented basketball players whose earnings didn't match Elvin's. Not surprisingly, some of them were predicting that Big E would fall flat on his face in the big league. It looked as though his doubters were at least partly right at the beginning of that 1968-69 season. In one game, against the massive barrier that is Wilt Chamberlain, Elvin was outfoxed and boxed out by Wilt and the other large Lakers, and by game's end he showed only nine rebounds to the Big Dipper's 23. The only consolation Elvin could take from the game was that Wilt had outscored him by only five points, 28 to 33. But the rebounding statistics apparently told all there was to tell: no rookie center rates as a superstar when he pulls down a measly nine rebounds in a game.

Even Jack McMahon, then Elvin's coach on the San Diego Rockets, called it the worst game Elvin had played. But McMahon quickly added, "His problem is learning the league. Watch him when he comes back."

So everybody watched the 6'9½", 235-pound bonus baby, including those who were hoping he'd go from so-so to oh-no. But not every center in the NBA is Wilt Chamberlain—7'1" and 275 pounds—who can stop an opposing center by just leaning on him or intimidating him with an awesome combination of strength and savvy. And apart from Wilt and Bill Russell—in his final year—enemy centers found Elvin to be quite a force. Nate Thurmond couldn't stop him, Bob Rule came out second best in their duels, and so it went around the league. Two nights running Big E hit for 40 points against the Chicago Bulls, then upped his scoring grades with 54 against the Detroit Pistons. His basket-making binge went on with 38 against Chamberlain's Lakers, 33 against the defense-minded New York Knickerbockers and Willis Reed, 37 and 39 against the Philadelphia 76ers, 32 against the shot-throttling talents of Bill Russell and the Boston Celtics. And the uncertain newcomer who had started slowly had turned the corner, scoring and rebounding with a sureness that seemed to declare, "I'm not falling on my face. I'm here to stay."

The 1968-69 season went into the books with Elvin Hayes having joined the ranks of the mighty with the kinds of statistics that impress even the harshest "show-me" die-hards. His 2,327 points and 28.4 average were No. 1 in the NBA, and his 1,406 caroms, which averaged out to 17.1 rebounds per game, put him behind just three other pivotmen—Chamberlain, Russell, and Westley Unseld. Yet, even though his point barrage made him only the second rookie ever to win the scoring title (there's Chamberlain again, first to earn that distinction), Unseld won the Rookie-of-the-Year award. The rebuff by the voters rankled Elvin, who said, "Time will bear out who is the better player—Wes or me." There were many others who shared E's viewpoint, underscoring the fact that Unseld had a much better setting for his talents (the Baltimore Bullets had won the Eastern Division championship even though Elvin had done more as an individual than Wes. When confronted with a comparison between himself and Hayes, Unseld refused to measure himself against the Rockets' rookie. "We are different types of players," the Baltimore center said. "I admit that Elvin is more spectacular, and he's a great athlete. I've believed him to be that from the first minute I saw him in action."

Taking into consideration that the Rockets of last season were nowhere near comparable to the Bullets, there is no valid way to compare Hayes and Unseld as contributors to their respective teams. But the statistics for last year do show a vast difference between them as sophomores on the basis of individual comparison. Playing for a third-place team, Wes finished with an average of 16.7 rebounds (second best in the NBA) and a scoring average of 16.2 points per game. The league's leading rebounder was Hayes, with 1,386 caroms and a 16.9 per-game average. And while his scoring diminished slightly in comparison to his rookie season, Elvin's 2,256 points and 27.5 average earned him third place in the scoring race. In the numbers game alone, Elvin outdistanced Wes by a good margin. It lends additional support to the argument of those who thought Hayes deserved the Rookie-of-the-Year award, and it reinforces Elvin's question about that award not being his: "Don't they notice what I do out there?" he asked at the end of his freshman season. "Doesn't the box score count for anything?"

It certainly counted enough for Elvin to be named to the All-Star team in each of his two pro seasons. And it has always counted since his days as a high-school basketball player. But what people say and think about him also count a lot to Hayes. It's been that way for him since he was a youngster growing up in his home town of Rayville, Louisiana. The 24-year-old star can look back at his childhood in that small town and remember almost nothing but physical and mental pain.

Elvin was the sixth and last child of Chris and Savannah Hayes, a youngster who was constantly ridiculed by everyone outside his house. As he recalls those early years of his life, the only person who really loved him was his father, and Chris Hayes died of a heart attack when Elvin was in the ninth grade. In this regard, Elvin told Arnold

Hano, for a *Sport* Magazine article, "As a kid, people would say to me, 'You'll never be anything.' Pretty soon I stopped caring about being anything. I stayed close to myself. People thought I was real stupid. I didn't run around with the other kids. I didn't talk to them. I was real quiet."

Hayes became an "outsider" partly because of the speech defect that made it impossible for him to pronounce certain words. It is a problem he has almost completely overcome (he concentrated on speech therapy while attending Houston University), although an attentive listener can detect certain imperfections in his speech even now. However, back then teachers weren't too sympathetic to his problem and the other kids were plain cruel. Hayes's memory of the cruelty of his peers is exemplified by an incident involving three older boys who attacked him one day, slamming his head against a floor, bloodying and bruising his face with their fists. The physical hurt was terrible, but the feeling passed in the following days. What time hasn't cured is the mental pain inflicted by that attack. In some deep way it must symbolize all the torment and depressive suffering childhood represented to Hayes.

Fortunately, he found escape from the dreariness of Rayville—in basketball. When he first tried to make his school team, he proved too clumsy. But the coach encouraged him to keep at it. He did, practicing for hours by tossing a rubber ball into a tin can. His marksmanship improved and his clumsiness was replaced by fine coordination and a smooth swiftness on the basketball court. Hayes's scoring, rebounding and physical strength impressed scouts and he accepted the scholarship offered by Houston University. One of the better opportunities it afforded him was to get away from the bad memories of Rayville.

Suddenly the home-towners weren't so eager to get rid of "stupid Elvin," and they tried to dissuade him from going to Houston. "All of the people in my home town who wanted me to go to one of the big Negro colleges in Louisiana told me I wouldn't be truly accepted in Houston," Elvin recalls. "They said the people at Houston would just use me. They said they wouldn't be interested in me as a person, just as a basketball player. They said that when my white teammates walked off the court, they wouldn't know me."

On the contrary, as it turned out, Elvin was well known on and off the court. At Houston he roomed with a white boy, encountered little racial discrimination, and met the girl he was eventually to marry. (Today, he, Erna and Elvin Hayes, Jr., live in an $82,000 home in La Jolla, California). And so prolific were Hayes's talents with a basketball that he put little-known Houston on the national basketball map. In his freshman year he smashed every first-season record at the University, which brought these words of praise from freshman coach Harvey Pate: "I've been around basketball players for 22 years and I've never seen anything like Elvin. He's big, powerful, and springy. On defense he's like Bill Russell. He just hangs around the basket and stuffs shots back in the shooter's face."

Sophomore Hayes broke almost all of the varsity records, including the one-season mark for scoring with a 27.2 per-game average. He bettered that in his junior year, popping in points at an average of 28.4 per game. And he went himself several better as a senior, driving the average to 36.4 points per game. As his varsity coach said of Elvin, the graduating senior, "If there's any college basketball player better than Elvin, I've never seen him."

Hayes had come a long way from his sad beginning in Rayville. The home-town folks thought a lot more of him now than any of them could ever have imagined possible. And at least equally as important to Elvin was what the pros thought of him, when he became available for pro ball. The ABA's Houston Mavericks tempted the All-America with a reported $300,000 for three years, but that bid didn't meet the attractiveness of the San Diego contract that added up to $440,000. Yet, more important than the money, as far as Elvin was concerned, was the difference in competition he would meet in the ABA and the NBA. The NBA got his nod because he "never once thought of playing in the American Basketball Association, no matter how much they offered," since he wanted to go against the best.

How he has played against the best in his two seasons is shown in his statistics and the accolades he has earned from coaches and players. Arnold "Red" Auerbach, Boston Celtics general manager, said, "Hayes has that beautiful body. He's just as strong at the end of a game as he is at the beginning." Another coach remarked, "With another team Elvin wouldn't have to carry such a load, having to score and rebound and play so many minutes. With a better team he'd be right up there in the running for Most Valuable Player, because a player's team record is what influences a lot of voters. Even so, Hayes is practically a one-man team right now."

Those are the kind of words reserved for stars like Chamberlain, Reed and Alcindor. Is superstar Hayes fated to suffer because San Diego doesn't have the guns to make it big? Not if Big E can help it. He's overcome tougher problems than that.

SPENCER HAYWOOD

In the bidding wars that have escalated players' contracts into the million-dollar class, the NBA has annually outclassed the ABA. Maravich, Lanier, Alcindor ... almost all of the cream of the college crops have settled down with a senior-league team. And until the two loops merge—an any-day possibility which could be taking place while this is being written—one of the few who got away from the NBA will never know just how well he'd do against the best basketball players of all. That one is Spencer Haywood, who was kidnapped, the NBA says, out of Detroit University before he was eligible for the pro draft. The ABA claimed they came by Haywood's services honestly; they maintained the eligibility rule didn't apply to him since he proved a claim of "hardship." According to an ABA bylaw, Haywood qualified because he fitted the definition: "In cases of extreme hardship, a player may be signed before his class graduates."

At the time of his decision to leave college for pro ball, Haywood was scoring at a 31.8 points-per-game pace and leading all collegiate rebounders with a 21.5 per-game retrieve mark. The reported amount he received for signing was $250,000, although Haywood insisted, "It's a lot more than that—a lot more." He also insisted that he, not the ABA, made the initial contact with the Denver Rockets. "I consulted my high-school coach and legal guardian, Will Robinson, in Detroit, before going to negotiate."

Haywood cited his family's difficulties as the underlying motivation for his move. "I was tired of other people taking over my responsibilities," he said. "I've got four sisters and five brothers and my father died before I was born. My mother raised us all and she's worked long enough." He also recalled his childhood. "When I was 10 or 11, I didn't have a thing, not a thing. My mother did everything she could but it was a big family. I want to help others as well as myself."

Among the people he helped most—and immediately—were the Denver Rockets. In his first game he was in a rough test situation, facing the defending ABA champions, the Washington Caps. The 6'9", 235-pound rookie center played uncertainly at first, then started pouring it on. He hit the boards hard and often, sweeping rebounds with powerful hands and zipping passes to teammates geared to fast-break play. As he ruled the boards, fans were reminded of his stated desire to be as much like Bill Russell as he could. "Russell has been my hero for as long as I can remember," the 21-year-old strongman said. "I've read his books on basketball and everything he's said that I could find. I've followed his career since I was old enough to read. He's my idol. The thing is, I've got to assume his responsibility on defense. It's something that will take time, but that's what I'm aiming for."

He was already doing that, and far surpassing his idol in the offense department. On the attack he darted and bounced, fighting for and winning good position under the opponent's basket, putting in two-pointers with regularity. Behind the Caps by 11 points in the third quarter of his break-in game, Haywood led a Denver resurgence that brought them back in the fourth quarter and carried them past Washington, 106-105. The "hardship case" had made his presence felt with strong rebounding and a solid 24 points, most by a Rocket player.

There was no letdown in his second game. Haywood again led all Denver scorers with 22 points, and set a team rebounding record by coming away with 26 caroms. He was also repaying the Rocket investment in him by drawing fans by the thousands all around the circuit. And by maintaining his fantastic rookie pace in rebounding and scoring (he was switched to forward early in the season, not that it made a difference), he kept the crowds coming, strengthening his argument with the Denver front office that he deserved more money. The Rockets' money man agreed by April of last season, and Haywood inked a new six-year contract that put him in the $1.9-million Pete Maravich earning league.

Almost two-million dollars is a lot of money for someone with Haywood's checkered background. In his early teens Spencer was living with his family in Silver City, Mississippi, and dropping into school only when he had nothing better to do. Somehow, he managed to graduate from high school, even though he paid no more attention to schoolwork in Chicago and Detroit, where he periodically lived with relatives. His capsule description of himself is, "I was, you know, a thug. All I wanted to do was rob, or hustle a pool game, whatever it took to make some money." Hardly admirable, but at least more honest than a number of other "good guy" athletes who begin to believe all the marvelous things the publicity machines grind out about them. One of the major factors to influence Haywood away from a life in the streets was a man named Will Robinson. Robinson, formerly the basketball coach at Detroit's Pershing High School, met Haywood and took an interest in his welfare. Haywood responded and soon Robinson had arranged for a Detroit couple with three children of their own to provide the 15-year-old wanderer with a legal residence. "He was so poor and backward," said Mrs. Ida Bell, the woman of Haywood's new home. "Since his family couldn't help, we tried to love him as ours."

The attention of Mr. and Mrs. Bell plus the friendship and coaching of Will Robinson diverted Haywood from the gutter world to school and basketball courts. Fame and accomplishments convinced him there was more to life than being "a thug." Under Robinson he became an All-America high-school player and, in his senior year, repaid Robinson by driving Pershing High to the Michigan state championship. He next followed Robinson's advice and enrolled at Trinidad Junior College, in Colorado, where his average of 27 points and 23 rebounds a game brought him an invitation to try out for the 1968 U.S. Olympic squad. He made it and proved to be a leading force in the successful U.S. defense of its Olympic record of perpetual dominance over the world's best amateur basketball teams. Coach Hank Iba, who supervised the team in Mexico City, had nothing but good things to say about the Detroit youngster. "Haywood is so sincere, I can't believe it," Iba said. "He's always the first man across the floor to shake hands with the other team, and he's our hardest worker. He could make it now with most pro clubs."

That was precisely the impression he made on basketball fans who saw him in action for the University of Detroit the next year. Writer Mike O'Hara described him as one of college's kings of the court. "The huge, ominous figure soared high into the air," O'Hara pictured Spencer, "blocked the smaller opponent's shot and, in the same motion, snatched the basketball out of the air. He then dribbled the ball the length of the court—his mammoth strides carrying him swiftly toward the opposite end of the court. He gripped the ball like a grapefruit and then, with one vicious swing of his arm, slammed it through the basket with such force that the rim was torn off the backboard and the backboard itself was shattered in a thousand powdery pieces."

That was Haywood's first game for Detroit, the basket didn't count because dunking isn't allowed in college, and it didn't matter as far as the game was concerned, anyway—Detroit was leading 105-40. But it did prove there was another center playing college ball besides Lew Alcindor and Bob Lanier.

After a demonstration like that, Spencer was considered ready to carry the Detroit team to heights above even those reached by the teams on which Dave DeBusschere had starred several years before. And it seemed to be working out that way as Haywood powered the varsity squad to win after win that saw their stock rise nationally. At one point they were ranked seventh in the country in Haywood's first season. Then Detroit started losing some games, and the next thing to stun the school, Spencer's coach, and the NBA was the news that Haywood was joining the Denver Rockets.

Haywood's great show of strength at the beginning of

his rookie season was just a hint at what he would do before the 1969-70 schedule ended. In a game against the Los Angeles Stars, Haywood did so much for the Rockets that play-by-play announcer Sam Balter declared, "Spencer Haywood is on his way to developing into the perfect player. He's a composite of all those people we call superstars. I've actually seen him leap and intercept a field-goal try more than twenty feet away from the basket. Nobody else has ever done that. Haywood is the best jumper in the history of the game."

Haywood added more glory to his freshman fame in the ABA All-Star game. Playing head-to-head against Mel Daniels, the league's 1968-69 MVP, Spencer snared 19 rebounds to Daniels' 12, and outscored Mel 23 to 13. Spencer's contributions led his West team to a 30-point win and earned him the MVP award.

By the end of the regular season, Denver had taken the Western Division title and Spencer Haywood had gathered honors galore. He scored the most points of any player in the ABA, 2,519, and topped the scoring averages with a 29.9 per-game mark. He also hauled down the most rebounds, 1,637, and had the best rebounding average, 19.4 per game. And in the course of ringing up all those points, he broke the single-game scoring mark of 57 points, set by Connie Hawkins as an ABAer, by streaming in 59 points against the L.A. Stars. So not a soul was shocked when Haywood took home two trophies at the close of last year—one for Rookie of the Year and one for Most Valuable Player in the ABA. And since his total points, total rebounds and rebounding average all set new league records, the MVP will be out to break his own marks this year. Is there anyone in the ABA who can stop him?

LOU HUDSON

Contrary to most movie, television and book scripts, real-life heroes are not quiet, self-effacing souls with a deep reluctance to talk about their great deeds. In reality,

LOU HUDSON,
Atlanta Hawks' guard (UPI)

WILT CHAMBERLAIN,
Los Angeles Lakers' center

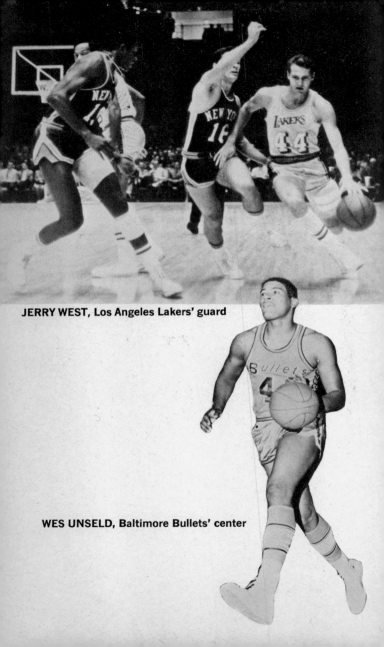

JERRY WEST, Los Angeles Lakers' guard

WES UNSELD, Baltimore Bullets' center

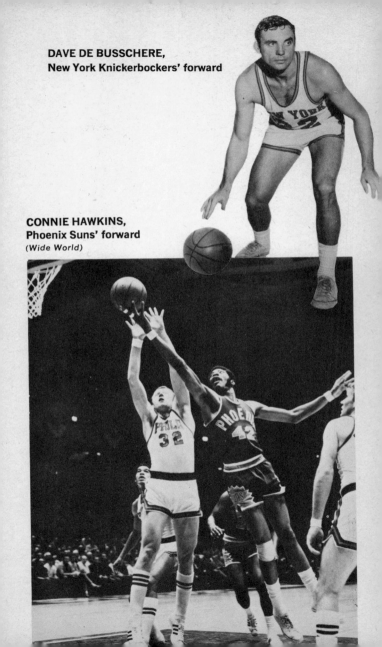

DAVE DE BUSSCHERE,
New York Knickerbockers' forward

CONNIE HAWKINS,
Phoenix Suns' forward
(Wide World)

SPENCER HAYWOOD,
Denver Rockets' center
(*Sport Magazine*)

PETE MARAVICH,
now with Atlanta Hawks, guard

LEW ALCINDOR,
Milwaukee Bucks' center

OSCAR ROBERTSON,
now with Milwaukee Bucks,
guard *(UPI)*

EARL MONROE, Baltimore Bullets' guard

WALT FRAZIER,
New York Knickerbockers' guard

JOHN HAVLICEK,
Boston Celtics' forward

WILLIS REED,
New York Knickerbockers'
center *(Martin Blumenthal)*

ELVIN HAYES,
San Diego Rockets' center

BILLY CUNNINGHAM,
Philadelphia 76ers' forward

Printed in U.S.A.

there are often loud-mouthed characters who love adoration and publicity. Then along comes a Lou Hudson, the strong, silent type who performs heroics off and on basketball courts and modestly plays down his accomplishments. And you start to believe in fiction again.

Take the time Lou was starring for John Kundla at the University of Minnesota. In his first game as a sophomore, Lou's Gopher team was battling Purdue and each Big Ten five wanted the win badly enough to commit mayhem. It looked like the Boilermakers had succeeded at exactly that when Hudson, fighting for the ball on a rebound, slammed his head against the backboard. The *crack* of the collision cut short the excited shouts of the crowd, and the sound of his body slamming to the floor echoed through the silent arena. Kundla and the Gophers' trainer rushed to his side but Lou simply got up, shook off the pain, had the injury treated right there, and stayed in the game. Actually, he more than stayed in the game, he *was* the game as he bombarded the basket for 15 of Minnesota's next 20 points. Behind the fire and firepower exhibited by Hudson, the Gophers overtook Purdue and notched an important victory.

Another Big Ten contest, in Lou's senior year at Minnesota, was the scene for even greater heroics on Hudson's part. The first act in the drama had been performed in the fifth game of the season, when Lou broke his arm in another hustle situation that brought out his best efforts. The arm was placed in a cast and he was warned not to play for a minimum of two months. That sounded like solitary confinement to Hudson, and he refused to accept the medical verdict. "I just kept on going to practice," he said, "and begging the coach to let me play. Finally, I convinced him I could handle the ball with the cast on." Faced with such spirit and determination, the coach had to give Lou a chance, especially since Minnesota had a "must" game with Indiana coming up, and Lou might be able to help a little.

Wearing a slightly lighter cast, Hudson manipulated the ball—passing, dribbling, shooting—by using the cast-weighted right hand to support his left hand. And his "little" contribution added up to 20 points on a 50 percent shooting average.

Nobody who witnessed Hudson's show of team spirit

and play under such conditions will ever forget it. But to anyone who knew him, it was typical of the Hudson approach to life, dating back to his high school days. Then he did his quiet hero act for coach Bill Furcron at Dudley High School in Greensboro, North Carolina. "In high school," Hudson recalled, "I used to feel nobody could shoot better than I. That's not bragging, I was just confident. And this feeling kept my interest in basketball. Until the ninth grade I had switched sports with the seasons: I played football, baseball and basketball. But I stopped playing baseball in the ninth grade and only played basketball from the end of one football season to the beginning of the next. For some reason, I originally wanted to play football the most. And although it's been written that I was a great high-school quarterback, the truth is, I wasn't. It was Mr. Furcron who convinced me my best future was in basketball."

Now one of the tallest and heaviest of the NBA guards, 6'5", 220-pound Lou moves with the grace and agility of a man three inches shorter and 40 pounds lighter. And he attributes much of his smoothness and maneuverability to habits developed under Coach Furcron's tutelage. "Mr. Furcron perfected a drill and insisted I practice it over and over. In fact, I still practice it," Hudson said. "He would pair me against a guard every chance he got, and I was a forward at the time. This kind of pairing resulted in the development of quickness which now equalizes things when I'm matched against someone bigger than I am"—which occurs not only against the new NBA forwards who exceed Lou in height, but also when he comes face to face with the league's centers.

It was his speed and mobility combined with basket-making and rebounding that brought Dudley High a clutch of titles, including the state's Negro high-school championship. His skills also brought him to the attention of Irwin Smallwood, in those days the Executive Sports Editor of the Greensboro *Daily News*. Smallwood remembered his first impression of Hudson in motion with these words: "Louis would get the rebound, bring it down court, shoot, score, and go back for another rebound. He scored 20 points in the first 16 minutes I saw him play. He reminded me of Tom Gola, Doug Moe, those guys who were the first of the smoothies."

Hudson was also a model of the modern athletic idol away from the basketball court. When he wasn't going one-on-one with his schoolbooks, involved in school activities or helping with chores around his parents' house, he was earning money by shining shoes at a downtown shoestand. Such virtue—and basketball talent—couldn't go unrewarded, and Irwin Smallwood's one-man publicity job on Lou brought him statewide fame and offers from a number of colleges. Lou chose Minnesota.

In his seasons as a Gopher in that cold section of the country, Lou's shooting hand never lost its hot touch. In his junior season Hudson topped the Big Ten in field goals scored and posted a single-season mark on the basis of 588 points for a 23.3 points-per-game average. Additional honors accorded the youngster the pros now call Sweet Lou included three years as a member of the All-Big Ten squad, and one as All-America. And the only thing that short-circuited his assault on the all-time Minnesota scoring record—which he missed by a slim six points—was the broken arm he suffered in his senior year. All of which explains why Richie Guerin picked Hudson first for the then St. Louis Hawks at the 1966 professional college draft.

Hudson immediately made it clear he was a comer in the NBA. Playing at forward for 80 games in 1966-67, Lou scored at an 18.4 clip, leading all Hawk scorers and coming in second to Dave Bing in the voting for Rookie of the Year.

The U.S. Army limited his play to 46 games in the 1967-68 season, and an out-of-shape Hudson could manage only 12.5 points a game. He did salvage something for the season, though, when he came alive in six playoff games for a 21.7 average.

The scene was different the following year. The Hawks were based in Atlanta and Hudson was becoming what Baltimore's assistant coach Bob Ferry considered, "basketball's greatest offensive machine." On the strength of a 49.2 shooting average—which netted him 1,770 points and a 21.9 points-per-game mark—Lou was gaining the reputation of "another Jerry West." It had been only his second full season, but his shooting had gained him 15th place in the league scoring derby.

Yet, in spite of his marksmanship and totals, a teammate complained, "Lou doesn't shoot as much as we'd like him to. He connects on nearly half his shots, so he should take more. He seems kinda shy, like he's afraid someone is going to call him a gunner."

Lou, who is a shy, quiet person by nature, disagreed in his modest way. "If you're a scorer like me," he said, "you need to make a high percentage of your shots. If you don't, your teammates might wonder if they shouldn't be shooting themselves, instead of passing off to you."

Atlanta's coach, Richie Guerin, was also of the opinion that Lou should be shooting more. And one way, Guerin figured, to get him to do that was to have him handle the ball more. So, in the 1969 playoffs he decided to experiment with Hudson, his All-Star forward, at guard. In the first playoff game against the Los Angeles Lakers, Hudson had to test himself by facing no less a star than Jerry West. And West, normally a killer in playoffs (which is only slightly more than what he is during regular-season play), was beaten in head-to-head competition with Sweet Lou. In four games Hudson held him to a shooting percentage of 34 percent and a total of 75 points. In those same four games, Lou hit on close to 50 percent of his shots and rang up a total of 92 points.

"That did it for me," Guerin declared. "From then on, he was a guard."

Although Lou had to adjust to the new position, it wasn't too hard since backcourt play fitted well with his philosophy of basketball. "I'd rather take a man one-on-one and beat him," he said, "or watch a teammate do it. That's one of the things that make this a really fine game."

And even though he had to take on the slick ones like West, Walt Frazier, Oscar Robertson, et al., Hudson surprised even himself with the results. One of those results came in November of the 1970 season, when Lou took a huge (for him) total of 34 shots in a game against the Chicago Bulls—and hit on 25 of them. That boils down to nearly 75 percent success! "How do you stop a guy like that?" moaned Chicago coach Dick Motta after Lou finished the night with 57 points. Not only was it the high point of his scoring career, it matched the long-standing Hawk single-game mark set by the great Bob Pettit. Oh, yes—in addition, Lou had eight assists.

In the locker room after the game, Hudson's backcourt partner Walt Hazzard stated, "In time Lou is going to be the best ballplayer in this league. Right now, Lou's better than Jerry West, although Jerry's got a few years more behind him and has been injured a lot."

Part of what may have influenced Hazzard was Hudson's showing compared to West, as Lou and Jerry teamed up in backcourt for the West squad in the 1969-70 All-Star game. Over 31 minutes of court time, West tallied 22 points; in just 18 minutes of play, Hudson hit for 15. Statistically, Hudson won that confrontation hands down, and it moved another West squad player to comment, "Sweet Lou's superior to Jerry. Of course, Lou's a few years younger. But you really have to hound him, crowd him all the time. If you don't, he'll shoot you dead. He can hit on just about any shot twenty feet or less from the basket—and he's almost as deadly from more than twenty, too! If we had those three-point baskets like they do in the ABA, Lou's points would really go up."

By the end of this past season, guard Lou Hudson had won a spot on the All-NBA team. He did it on the strength of 2,031 points in 80 games, for a 25.4 points-per-game average, good for fifth place in the individual scoring race; a .531 field-goal percenage, third best in the NBA; and a free-throw percentage of .824, seventh in the league.

Yet, even though he's getting more and more national publicity, he continues to get things done without making a big splash while doing it. This quality was pointed up by an incident following a Hawk victory over Los Angeles. After the game Skip Caray, the Atlanta play-by-play announcer, came into the Hawk dressing room and announced, "I gotta start writing Lou's name on my sleeve." Someone asked why, and he said, "Here's the real Lou Hudson . . . on my statistics sheet. You remember Gary Gregor moving around a lot, and Davis on some layups, and Caldwell stealing the ball. So the game's over and you start to recap it and you say, 'Leading the Hawks were Gary Gregor and Jimmy Davis with 19 points apiece, Joe Caldwell with 15—' And then you look down and you say, "Er, ah, incidentally, folks, Lou Hudson had 25 points.' You don't even remember he was out there."

But his opponents always do.

PETE MARAVICH

No rookie entering the National Basketball Association has ever enjoyed a greater reputation than Pete Maravich. For three years before being drafted by the Atlanta Hawks, Pistol Pete was the rage of the sports pages, getting at least as much coverage as Lew Alcindor while playing for an LSU team that was far inferior to the college kings of UCLA. Pete was a three-ring circus, a Fourth of July fireworks display, a one-man festival of fun, fast basketball and fine shooting. Dribbling and passing, he out-Cousied Cousy. "Pete Maravich is doing things with a basketball Bob Cousy never dreamed possible," wrote Peter Finney, in his book, *Pistol Pete*, "even though it's likely his skills will not be fully appreciated until he gets coast-to-coast exposure with the pros." Former LSU star Joe Dean observed that "Pete is regarded chiefly as a scorer, a pop-gun. But his real appeal, the thing that sets him apart, is not his shooting but his passing which, to borrow a word from the astronauts, is 'fantastic.' When he's playing with the pros, in a league that prohibits a zone defense, fans are going to get a look at a white Globetrotter."

Shooting, the 6'5", 200-pound ball of fire out-Oscared Robertson. Until the 1969-70 college basketball season ended, Oscar Robertson had held the record for most points scored by a major-college star with 2,973 points in three years of play, and a per-game average of 33.8 points over that three-year stretch. When Maravich wrapped up his three-season stint at LSU he had whipped home 3,667 points, for a varsity average of 44.2 points per game in 83 contests. Not only did his scoring feats earn him All-America selection all three years, it won him the title of Player of the Year for 1970. His best year, and one that may never be topped, was 1970, when he became college basketball's first point-a-minute scorer by putting in 1,381 points in 31 games, for a 44.5 ppg mark. Finally, he set those records while maintaining a three-year shooting percentage of .447.

Pete has been described in many ways. The title of "ball hog" has been hung on him as it has always been hung on the great players by critics who delight in knocking the stars more out of reflex anger than reflective analysis. But no player can be as bad as all that if a pro team like Atlanta is willing to pay him a reported $1.9 million for his signature on a contract. They are in the camp that praises Pistol Pete as the gun that won the South, the skinny backcourt whiz who amazes with speed, strength and startling changes of pace to maneuver his way in and out of some of the weirdest situations ever to occur on a court. Adolph Rupp, the Kentucky coach who has seen some of basketball's best in action, describes Maravich "as near a complete ballplayer as you'll see anywhere." To which Frank McGuire adds, "Maravich can do everything with a basketball. He *can* pass. And he *can* score. He got 55 against Kentucky, and you know Rupp's teams always play good defense."

Bob Ferry, assistant coach and scout for the Baltimore Bullets, assessed precocious Pete's pro prospects by saying: "Pete should be a better pro—though not statistically—than he was a college player. He's got the ability to complement everyone else on the floor. He can move a club. He's a better passer than shooter. There are two kinds of players—those who go out and get great statistics and those who get statistics as well as make everyone else's stats better. Maravich fits into the second category." Then Ferry really warms up. "Maravich has the greatest basketball imagination I've ever seen. I simply don't know how he does half the things he does with the ball. He has great quick hands, quick eyes, he's an unbelieveable passer, and a great middleman on the fast break. He can penetrate with the ball, he can hit the open man— offensively, I don't think there's a thing he can't do. I saw Cousy a lot. I played with him. But I think this kid is a much better ballhandler. There's no comparison as far as dribbling and doing things with the ball. He's simply unbelievable."

In many ways, Maravich was born to play basketball. His father (and his coach at LSU), Press Maravich, was a fine basketball player himself, and he gave Pete as much encouragement to play as is humanly possible. From the day Pete entered the world—June 22, 1948—the elder Maravich surrounded him with basketball, talking, playing, watching. It was a non-stop education, day in, day out, year after year. In Pete's words, to Curry Kirkpatrick of *Sports Illustrated*, "I guess I love the game of basketball more than anything else in the world. From the beginning it was like an addiction with me, I played it so much. Forty-seven weeks out of the year. Four to five hours a day. I never really was interested in other sports or anything else, either. For a while I ran some track. But I could never see running around in a circle for a long time and just getting tired. Really, it was all basketball. The fact that my father, Press, was coaching the game probably had the most to do with it. I mean, if he had put a football in my hand I would have wanted to be a football player."

But basketball it was. In the Maravich back yard, at the local "Y", as a grade-schooler, at Daniel High School in Clemson, South Carolina, at Needham-Broughton High in Raleigh, Edwards Military Academy in Salemburg, North Carolina, and Louisiana State University. Even in movie theaters, where young Pete took an aisle seat so he could dribble and watch the show at the same time—and amuse the other movie patrons who evidently didn't mind the tap-tap-tap accompaniment to their film fare.

By junior-high school Pete-the-Tricky-Showman had been born. Taking on boys five and six years his senior, Pete would dominate the court, dribbling through his legs, swishing it around his back, passing "blind" with deadly accuracy, scoring at will. And winning the bemused attention of fans wherever he played. By the time he hit high school, the cool, clever moves were as much a part of his court repertoire as his professional touch and scoring ability. From that time, there was no other way for Press's boy to play the game of round ball. "I began throwing wilder passes and connecting with them," Pete recalled. "The crowds were getting bigger then, and once I had the people behind me, I wanted to do more and more with the ball. I remember one game I threw a behind-the-back bounce pass on the move through a guy's legs! I mean, man you understand? A behind-the-back through his legs! Oh, whoa! O remember I was coming down on a three-on-one break, and my man was overplaying me to the left and giving me the open teammate on the right. But that was too easy a pass. We were going to get two anyway, so it didn't make any difference. As my man was sliding and I was dribbling, I noticed his legs moving in and out, in and out. Still on the move, I saw the right moment and threw the ball when his legs were out—behind my back, now, not a straight pass—and I put it right through him to a teammate on the left. He converted for the basket. The crowd, boy. The crowd, I want to tell you, went berserk. I couldn't believe it. My man looked like somebody stepped on his head."

And therein lies one of the flaws in the near-ideal backcourt machine joining the Atlanta Hawks. To say that Richie Guerin will have his hands full taming the tempestuous applause-lover is no more an understatement than to say Wilt Chamberlain has been a coach's headache since before he entered the pros . . . and ever after. To Guerin, a very team-minded man, Pistol Pete must represent the greatest challenge of his life. Words to the effect that Maravich may not be the greatest thing to hit the pros, precisely because of his attitude, have been spoken almost as often as the praise that preceded his entry into the NBA. One voice in the anti-Maravich camp belonged to K.C. Jones, the former backcourt star of the Boston Celtics. K.C. referred to Pete's basket-gunning as "saturation shooting. He scores 50 points but throws up 100 shots." And with Atlanta being blessed with the high-scoring and highly accurate Lou Hudson at one backcourt slot, and play-making standout Walt Hazzard at the other, Maravich will have to tone down his one-man show if he's going to reshape Guerin's thinking out the Hawk lineup. "I'm sure his shooting will become more realistic when he's a pro," said Joe Mullaney, coach of the Los Angeles Lakers, and a man who knows what *prima donna* problems can be—he had Wilt Chamberlain as his center last year. Obviously, something or someone has to give, because no ballplayer gets almost two million dollars for bench-warming. Which suggests that Guerin's biggest challenge may turn around to be Maravich's biggest challenge.

So, with the 1970-71 season underway, it's good luck to Richie Guerin, good luck to the Hawks, and good luck to the hot-headed, hot-shooting, hot-dogging pro freshman who said not too long ago, "I guess there are several tons of ham in me—that must be obvious—and I recognized early that basketball, more than any other team game, gives a guy the opportunity to be a showman. The skills involved in basketball are different. You can do more stuff, more antics. And one guy has much more leeway to put on a show. That really is what basketball is for me—an entertainment, a chance to express myself. It's what I've chosen to do in my life, it's my thing . . . I bet at least 90 percent of the people want to see my show. You can't tell me just 10 percent want it."

No . . . but Richie Guerin just may be in that ten percent. And then . . .???

EARL MONROE

The man of many moves was in motion again. He dribbled quickly down court, shifting his body in tempo to the tap-tap of the ball against the boards, advancing closer to the Knick basket as Walt Frazier's swift hands itched for a grab of the basketball. Then the dribbling stopped and the ball was snapped inside to Wes Unseld, who whipped it out to Gus Johnson, who pumped it right out again to the man who had brought it down. Earl Monroe took the pass, gave Frazier a couple of cute moves and arched his sinewy frame up and slightly back. Then he let fly and the shot skinned past the hoop for a clean two-pointer. A grin split Monroe's face as he back-pedaled on defense.

The moves of Earl Monroe varied throughout the seven-game playoff series between the Knicks and Baltimore Bullets last Spring. But one thing was constant, Earl the Pearl's steady stream of fire that kept the Bullets in game after game. It was his play, along with that of Gus Johnson and Wes Unseld, that nearly propelled the Bullets past the greatest Knick team of all time.

In the first game of that 1969-70 elimination series, Monroe bulls-eyed the nets for 39 points, on a 14 for 28 demonstration of sharpshooting from the floor and 11 for 14 from the foul line. The Knicks took the double-overtime scuffle, 120-118, but not because Monroe gave it to them. "That Monroe is unbelievable," was one of the first things Walt Frazier said in the New York locker room after the game. "I don't think The Pearl saw the basket on some of his shots, but he's that kind of shooter."

And, as proved by his close-to-30-points-a-game average, he's especially that kind of shooter when it's needed most. In the previous year's playoffs, against the same Knick team, it was Earl Monroe who piled up 113 points in the four-game series, for a 28.3 average. He had come to play—and he did!—but the Knicks couldn't be contained and blasted Baltimore into oblivion without losing a game.

So once more it's *wait until next year* for Baltimore's Bullets, and back with them will come the hope and optimism they had in '69 and '70. In fact, Kevin Loughery, Earl's running mate in the backcourt, is probably thinking the same thoughts he expressed before the 1969 season began. "Earl," Loughery said, "is the superstar we've been needing to compete with the other strong teams. Don't be surprised if he leads the league in scoring. It's not that I think we're a one-man club, it's just that, in clutch situations, it's only natural that we look for Earl to take charge, get the basket we need. If you need a big hoop in the last seconds, the best thing to do is clear a side for him."

While Monroe didn't lead the league in scoring last year, he didn't exactly embarrass his friends, relatives and teammates with his statistics. Ninth among the league's leading point-makers with a pretty respectable 23.4 per-game average, Earl managed to stay healthy for 82 games. And that, for The Pearl, is a medical marvel. He stands 6'3" and carries 190 pounds of finely tuned talent onto the floor, but carrying those 190 pounds are a pair of legs that could do with a quick transplant. At 26, Monroe has the underpinnings of a little old lady in tennis shoes. Indeed, it isn't stretching a point to say that he plays every game as if it could be his last. Both knees are arthritic, have bone chips and calcium deposits. "They are so bad," said Skip Feldman, the Bullets' trainer and traveling secretary, "that I've sometimes seen them puffed up so bad you could squeeze them like sponges."

That doesn't mean Monroe lets the aches and pains stop him or even slow him down, particularly in must-win contests. Even though the knees are almost always taped and Earl is limping from half-time on, when the game's pace and roughness really pick up, he not only matches the pace, he often sets it. "The doctor says it's just something I've got to live with," Monroe said realistically about the condition, "So I do."

Frank Deford, writing in *Sports Illustrated,* characterizes Monroe as a man who defies injury the way Superman defies bullets. "Gimpy, hobbling along like an arthritic old man until the game begins, he comes onto the court and suddenly is whole and strong and agile, as if touched by some faith healer. Renowned for his flash, he is actually the model of efficiency, controlling the ball, and with it the game and the crowd, until, with a whoosh of verve, he has made the play."

But unlike Superman, Earl doesn't take on the enemy single-handed. His move is often a pass to another man, rather than the crowd-pleasing pop-shot or acrobatic drive down the middle. A fan needn't look any farther than last year's Baltimore team statistics, which show Earl with 402 assists. If that doesn't seem impressive, consider that his nearest Baltimore rival in that department had only 292 assists.

Facts such as these account for what Baltimore scouts raved about and why the club paid the Winston-Salem graduate an estimated $200,000 bonus to sign in 1967. Earl started to develop into that valuable a player in Philadelphia, Pa., where he first began making a reputation as a soccer player. It wasn't until he broke a leg on the soccer field, at 14, that he turned his full attention to basketball, and tried out for his junior-high-school basketball team. To Earl's suprise, the basketball coach wasn't too impressed with him, so the teenager went to work to crack the varsity lineup. "Once I started," Monroe said, recalling his first serious attempts to play basketball, "I practiced every day, from early morning till dark, only quitting to eat lunch."

But, as Monroe learned, it's not the easiest thing to master a sport well enough to outdo other kids who had been playing since they were big enough to handle a basketball—especially not in Philadelphia, a hot-spot of basketball activity. In fact, it wasn't until he was a high-school junior that he broke into the team. Even then, he had to wait another season before he put it all together and, as a 6'2" center, posted a per-game scoring average of 21.7 to win a spot on the All-City team.

Perseverance had paid off and a batch of college scholarships came his way. But he wasn't sure if that was the route he wanted to follow. Instead of accepting a scholarship, he took a $60-a-week job as a shipping clerk. However, it wasn't long before he discovered that shipping clerks don't get cheers and don't make a fortune. So his next stop was Winston-State College in North Carolina.

It was clear that Monroe had really arrived as a court star when his polished play and point-making helped bring his team the NCAA College-Division championship in 1967. That attracted the pro scouts for a close inspection of the gem later to become The Pearl. Former pro Jack McMahon was among those scouts, and his report included the impression that Monroe "was the only college player in the last 15 years that I'd pay to see play again, and that includes Bill Bradley, Jimmy Walker and Lew Alcindor."

Considering what those three were like, it was hard to imagine what incredible feats Monroe must have displayed, so Gene Shue, his present coach, had to see for himself. What Shue witnessed was Monroe having an off-night, and he left the arena convinced that Earl didn't have the credentials to make the Bullets. "I thought he was letting the game get the better of him," Shue said disappointedly. "Frankly, I wanted no part of him."

Still, Shue was willing to take another look at Earl when he tried out for the 1967 Pan-American Games team. The turnaround in Monroe's play really impressed Shue, as Earl put on an all-around display of ball-handling, passing and scoring. Shue returned to Baltimore, sold on the cage star from Philadelphia, and he didn't learn until later that Monroe wasn't even selected to the team that went to the Pan-American Games!

Whoever made the choice to leave Earl behind must have hidden in a corner when Earl completed his fresh-man schedule as a Bullet. All he did in 1967-68 was get named Rookie of the Year and win unanimous election when the coaches picked the NBA's All-Rookie team. His impressive showing included 1,991 points scored, for an average of 24.3 over an 82-game schedule.

The next year he came back to play in 80 games and post a 25.8 per-game average, scoring 2,065 points. Earl was only one of three NBA players to exceed 2,000 points that year and was designated as a first-team selection on the All-NBA squad.

Monroe's three-year pro record of better than 24-points-a-game scored accounts for some of his value to the Baltimore franchise. But it's also his leadership qualities that bring the team to life that make him even more valuable to the club. As far as the fans are concerned, he's basketball's answer to the three-ring circus. Capitalizing on his flair for the dramatic, Earl dazzles them with show-stopping plays that bring out cries of admiration for his skills and laughs of pleasure at the ease with which he accomplishes these deeds. Bob Rubin, writing for *Sport* Magazine, said it this way: "Earl the Pearl. It fits. It has just the right show–business ring, because on a court Monroe is the consummate showman. He plays with a flair—the behind-the-back dribble, the Globetrotter pass and move, the body control that makes lies of the laws of natural science. Even the most devoted Pearl watchers, including his own teammates, miss parts of the show. [When Monroe is] driving for a layup, the ball is suddenly passed in a blur from one hand to the other behind his back. And what begins as a righthanded shot becomes a lefthanded shot, and it happens so fast people aren't sure how it happens. The crowd gasps at the speed of the move and the sheer audaciousness of it."

Showmanship? Yes. But there's plenty of pure basketball excellence going on at the same time. His coach has no complaints. Of Earl, Shue said, "He does all the things you want a guard to do." And Monroe, speaking of his offensive game with the pride and confidence typical of an athlete who believes in himself, said matter-of-factly, "I don't believe I can be stopped. The thing is, I don't know what I'm going to do with the ball, and if I don't know, I'm quite sure the guy guarding me doesn't know, either."

Walt Frazier and all the other guards in the NBA will say "Amen!" to that.

WILLIS REED

What the center of the Knicks had done all season long, serve as the kingpin of a finely tuned basketball machine, earned him fully deserved recognition. He won the designation as Most Valuable Player of the All-Star game. He was named MVP of the NBA for 1970. He could have been named Mayor of New York City except for certain legal procedures that kept that office in the hands of John Lindsay. Yet, on the strength of his regular-season play alone, thousands of New York Knick fans were convinced he had done more for Gotham than any public official. And his showing in the playoffs—against Baltimore, Milwaukee and Los Angeles—could have resulted in a power play for the Presidency. For Willis Reed was a physical and psychological force over those 19 contests which saw the Knicks run, shoot and defend their way to their first NBA title ever. "No man," wrote Frank Deford in *Sports Illustrated*, "had to face, in succession, the quality of opponents he has—Wes Unseld, last year's MVP; Lew Alcindor, next year's MVP; and Chamberlain, MVP two years ago and still a great bulwark even in active convalescence from knee surgery."

But it wasn't until the 19th and last game of the playoff series that Reed's full meaning to the Knicks was displayed. Injured, and injured badly, Reed had been kept out of the sixth game between L.A. and New York, a game which witnessed an L.A. rout of the Knicks and pointed up the key role Reed played in the New York team's success. And even though he had gotten four days of rest, plus treatment for muscle pulls and heavy doses of cortisone shots, Reed's participation in the deciding game was still doubtful when the two teams took the floor at Madison Square Garden. Then, seconds before the opening tap-off, Willis appeared. The sight of the 6-9, 235-pound pivotman caused several reactions: The 19,500 hometown fans exploded an ovation that sent wave after

wave of ecstatic joy cascading over Their Team. The
Knicks themselves seemed to grow inches in height and
actually seemed to glow with the jolt provided by the
Captain's presence. The Lakers stopped whatever they
were doing and just watched Willis move onto the court
and handle the ball. Psychologically, alone, the New
Yorkers gained a 10-point edge right there.

The game began with Reed losing the tap to Chamberlain, but that meant nothing . . . Willus pumped in his first
two shots and got the Knicks off to a 7-2 lead. The
Lakers—obviously stunned and still trying to adjust their
thinking and play—never were in the game thereafter.
No matter that Reed was dragging his bad leg behind him
as the action flowed up and down the boards; no matter
that he didn't make another point and was barely able to
match muscle with Wilt Chamberlain; no matter that he
left the game before the first half ended and played little
of the second half, replaced by Nate Bowman. He had
electrified the Knicks, shocked the Lakers, and fulfilled
the magical part he had played all year long as the leader
of 1970's team of destiny, basketball version.

Among the spectators who followed the Knicks through
the playoffs was Fred Hodby, Reed's coach when Willis
played for Grambling College. Watching Willis handle
Lew Alcindor reminded Hodby of Reed "back then."
Hodby recalled, "As a freshman Willis was a great mental
ballplayer. He had that and the shot then, and now he has
learned to adjust. Willis is as tough as he is smart. I used
to turn discipline on the team over to him. He won the
NAIA national title when he was a freshman center. He
believes in being tough. He'd hit people when they came
down the middle." And Hodby pointed out how Reed had
forced Alcindor away from the basket, opening the lane
for Dave DeBusschere to come through for points and
rebounds, doing the same for Walt Frazier, all the while
getting his share of baskets and caroms.

Oddly enough, as both Reed and Hodby remember,
Willis was really intent on a career in football, not basketball, when he was a youngster. He was an all-state end as
a high-school gridiron star in his hometown of Bernice,
Louisiana. But the basketball coach at West Side High
convinced him to try out for the team, and Hodby did the

rest at Grambling. The payoff came when the Knicks picked him in the 1964 college draft.

Rookie Reed looked as if he had solved the Knick problem at center, one that had been haunting them for years. He hit for 1,560 points and a 19.5 ppg average for 1964-65, and grabbed 1,175 rebounds, for an average of 14.7 per game. His freshman play earned him a place on the East squad in the All-Star game, and he was named Rookie of the Year. Even so, the Knicks acquired big Walt Bellamy before the next season, and Willis found himself at forward when his sophomore year began.

Willis had to make a difficult adjustment, relearning many of the ways of play that had won him praise and awards as a freshman center. He had to be more mobile; he had to learn to shoot from different angles, using different techniques; he had to alter his style of play both on offense and defense. Despite injuries all season long, he adjusted well enough to take down 883 rebounds and score at a 15.5 ppg average. The year ended with the conversion of Willis Reed, a success, and with his coach at the time, Dick McGuire, stating, "You couldn't get him from me for anything. Willis is quickly getting into the superstar class. He's the most valuable player on the club."

Described as a model of consistency, Reed turned in game after game of reliable statistics. In the 1966-67 season, he snared 1,136 rebounds and upped his scoring to a 20.9 points-per-game ratio. The next year was more of the same: 1,073 rebounds and 20.8 points per game. And in 1968-69 he registered 1,191 caroms and put the ball through the hoop at a 21.1 pace. It was also the year he returned to center.

Then last year, the year of the Knicks, Reed outdid his best efforts. He took down 1,126 rebounds and put in 1,755 points. His baskets earned him a 21.7 ppg average—the best of his six-year career—and made him top scorer on the team. It also earned him reams of praise in the sports columns, as typified by these words of Leonard Lewin, New York *Post* columnist, on Reed's right to the Most Valuable Player award: "It would be criminal if Reed did not win the MVP. He has had a great year. He has rebounded, played team defense, set the picks and scored. He is the heart of a team with the best record in the NBA. Willis has performed like an MVP and should not be penalized because Frazier and DeBusschere have been so good. That would be like ignoring what Bill Russell did simply because he had John Havlicek, Bob Cousy, Tommy Heinsohn and other outstanding teammates. In his own way Reed has done the Russell job for the Knicks and it would be a terrible injustice if his contemporaries didn't recognize it in their votes."

What Lewin and others also recognized was that all this might never have happened if Bellamy hadn't been traded for Dave DeBusschere. It converted the Knicks into the powerhouse that became 1970 champions, a powerhouse with the bulk of its strength centered around their iron-man pivot. Whereas Bellamy had shown moments of greatness enveloped by many more moments of sloth, Willis at center consistently added fire and strength to a squad burning with desire, mobility, youth and speed. As one coach commented, "If I had my choice, I'd take him over all the other forwards in the league. But then I'd play him at center." And win it all.

What is there about this man that makes him so much more than others who match him in height and weight. Why is he the MVP when compared to pros like Elvin Hayes, Wes Unseld and Wilt Chamberlain playing in the same league? One answer comes from Frank Blauschild, the Knicks' publicity director. "Reed is the greatest," said Blauschild. "He cooperates, he hustles, he gives you the big game every night." Another answer comes from Eddie Donovan, former Knick general manager but once Reed's coach. "Willis Reed," Donovan recalled about the Knicks' center when he was a newcomer to the pros, "is the only player I ever had who asked me for a rule book when he joined the team. He wanted to know exactly what he could do and couldn't do. He was something special." Still another comes from his teammate, Dick Barnett: "Willis comes to play every night. He is in a class by himself as a hard worker. For his size he has great agility and a beautiful outside touch. It is the combination of these things that make him a great player, but the biggest thing is he puts out every night." But the best answers of all come from Willis Reed. "The game is a challenge and an experience," he said. "When a man accepts a challenge and sets out to prove himself, he can get an evaluation of himself. And it's a shame if you don't gain the most of your potential. It's a shame if a man doesn't hustle. That hurts. It hurts when you see a guy who does not do what he can do." And along with the drive to live up to his potential is Willis's drive to win. "I'll never become accustomed to losing," he has said several times. "I always feel as though I've failed my coach, my team, and the customers, when we lose."

Willis is the Knick fixture at center now. The sun-like source of energy that makes his satellites glow. This season he will be defending his MVP crown, his All-NBA center rating, his position as captain of the world champions of basketball. Even with their loss of some of the supporting cast to the expansion draft, the Knicks retain the core of the team that wears the king's crown. And leading them into battle to keep the crown is Willis Reed, who promises not to let up now that he's achieved his long-desired goal of being a winner. With someone like Reed, that's just another challenge—to do it again, even better than before.

OSCAR ROBERTSON

Oscar Robertson, the shooter, was the subject under discussion, and the man doing the talking was Red Holzman, coach of the New York Knicks. "He can carry the load, if he has to, getting the points when they're really needed. That's the thing about Oscar, to my way of thinking. Everything he does, he does so easy. It looks natural, smooth. He flows. There is seldom even a look of particular strain on his face. I think if there was no such game as basketball when Oscar was growing up, he would have just instinctively wanted to dribble a big, round ball."

There is that basketball completeness about Oscar Robertson which makes it impossible to talk about one aspect of his game without it leading, naturally and unavoidably, into the total impression he makes. As Holzman starts with the shooter and is soon led to considering everything

Robertson does, another coach will start with Oscar's non-shooting talents and end up discussing his scoring genius: "You'll notice that Oscar never throws the ball so hard that a teammate will drop it. It's just easy enough for anyone to handle. He has such a soft touch. And the touch in passing and ball-handling is consistent with the soft, easy way he puts up a shot."

This game with the round ball has always come soft and easy to Oscar, and his tireless devotion to refining the feel and comfort he naturally had has tooled him into virtually everybody's choice as the best guard ever to play basketball. Red Auerbach, general manager and former coach of the Boston Celtics, called Oscar the best backcourt man ever, fully aware that Oscar's former coach at Cincinnati was Bob Cousy—and Cousy, in his career as a Celtic under Auerbach, was often adjudged the finest guard of them all. "Oscar is the greatest ever to play the backcourt," Auerbach stated flatly. "I do not mean to short-change Cousy, who played brilliantly for me. And it's not because Robertson is playing and Cousy is not, because I don't have a short memory. But Roberston has it all."

Cousy clearly didn't agree with Auerbach. As the freshman coach of the Royals last year, he worked hard to have Oscar traded and today Robertson would be a Baltimore Bullet instead of a Milwaukee Buck if he hadn't exercised his contractual right to veto the terms of any trade. "The trade was my decision," Cousy said when word of the possible move of Robertson to Baltimore got out and Royals fans besieged him with angry, threatening letters. "It's a dirty job," Cousy went on, "not a popular thing. I'm the villain, the bad guy. I've put everyone under a lot of pressure. But I won't shirk my duty. I came here to build a hustling, exciting, dedicated team, and it's my judgment alone that's involved."

So even though his judgment regarding the trade didn't bear fruit until the season ended, Cousy's shuffling of the Cincinnati personnel and his de-emphasis of Robertson as the key to success had a sharp effect on both the team's play and on the new role for the Big O. "The way I see it," Robertson said in midseason, "is that Cousy is trying to build for the future. He wants young players. I suppose that, at 31, I'm not what he considers a young player. I don't like it, but Bob is trying to create unselfish play. He's trying to get the ball inside and you do what the coach tells you."

For Robertson, personally, the year turned out to be one of the least successful of his career. His achievements for nine pro seasons (not counting last year) with the Royals showed a points-per-game average of 29.7; for the 1969-70 season he posted a low-for-him average of 25.3 points per game. And his lowest number of assists for a season had been the 633 he recorded in 1967-68—until this past year's 558 went into the book. Although he showed little sign of slowing up last season, Robertson sat out 13 games because of a reported groin injury, and put in only 2,865 minutes of playing time in 69 games; in 1967-68, a season of injuries, Oscar played in 65 games for 2,765 minutes—and racked up a 29.2 points-per-game mark.

The Royals could finish no better than fifth in the Eastern Division last year, which could only add fuel to Cousy's heated desire for "hustling, excited, dedicated" players to replace those with tired blood. His perseverance finally paid off with the transfusion that sent "ancient and weary" Oscar to join Lew Alcindor, and brought 6'1" Flynn Robinson and 6'8" Charlie Paulk to Cincinnati. Robinson, a 29-year-old guard, is an explosive scorer with questionable defensive ability; Paulk, a forward who stands 6'8" and was a Little All-American, is a rookie who was a member of the 1968 U.S. Olympic team.

Perhaps the hardest blow to Robertson last year was that it was the first time his name was not listed among the All-NBA players, first team. Until 1970 he was a first-team selection all of his nine seasons as a pro.

Since he joined the Royals in 1960, Oscar had scored 22,009 points, for a lifetime NBA average of 29.4 points per game. Only Wilt Chamberlain shows a higher career average. And coming into last season, Oscar was the No. 1 assist-maker in pro history, having surpassed Bob Cousy's record to achieve that distinction. Now his all-time total is 7,731 assists. Robertson also is the owner of the NBA record for the highest assists-per-game average for one season. He made the top of that list in 1964-65 for feeding off for 861 baskets in 75 games, which averaged out to 11.5 assists a game. That record was doubly remarkable because Big O also scored at a 30.4 ppg clip that same season.

Yet there are critics who join Cousy in refusing to acknowledge that Robertson is a team player. They point out that Cincinnati had never won a championship in the ten years Oscar was setting his records, implying that he was directly to blame for the Royals' failure. In doing this, they choose to ignore what Robertson has said—and proved—about his part as a team man. "What's the use of me scoring a lot of points when I'm supposed to be the playmaker? Oh, I know I can score, and I know there are times when a guard should score. But me scoring 40 or 50 points a night, what good would it do? You know how many shots I'd have to take, and I just don't think I'd be doing my part for the best interest of the team. I should set people up, not take all the shots."

His former teammate, all-star Jerry Lucas, who was traded to San Francisco after Cousy's arrival, also saw Oscar as a scorer who cut down on total points to play a total game. Of Robertson's shooting, Lucas said, "Oscar has such absolute control of the ball and his body that he can put a defender where he wants to with a fake, and if he can't he's so strong that he can muscle his way by him. Even if a big man covers him under the basket, he can get him going up and down with head and shoulder fakes so that Oscar is finally going up while the other guy's coming down. If Oscar ever really sets out to see how many points he could score in a single game, there's no telling how high he could go."

Playing as he did with the Royals, Oscar soared as high as everyone was predicting when he completed his college career as a three-time All-America at the University of Cincinnati. While there, he shattered all the major-college scoring marks, was the first player ever to lead major-college scoring both as a sophomore (984 points, 35.1 points-per-game average) and as a junior (978 points, 32.6 average). And until Pistol Pete Maravich tore the scoreboard to shreds for LSU, Oscar's 2,973 total points record was the best.

Oscar is more than just another "jock." In the words of Walter Paul, who has known Robertson since he played basketball for Crispus Attucks High School in Indianapolis, "People watch Oscar play basketball and it's easy for them to recognize the fact that here is a young man with tremendous athletic ability. But what a lot of those same people don't realize is that here, too, is a young man with high intelligence."

Robertson was a B student in the school of business administration at the University of Cincinnati, and he applies his mind to basketball the way he applied it to classwork. "Consider coming down on a 3-on-2 break," he once said in analyzing court strategy. "Generally the rule in basketball is that the middle man stops at the foul line if nothing else has developed so that you don't give the two defensive men the chance to cover all three of you. But instead of stopping there, why not go all the way in and try to create a situation? You may get a three-point play, and you may be able to get your man free under the basket, where if you just take the jump shot from the foul line, you only have a 50 percent chance of it going in."

Applying the sum of his talents and intelligence to basketball has gained 6'5", 220-pound Oscar Robertson a yearly salary that reached the $125,000-a-year range with the Royals. Now it is reported to be $175,000 a year. But the one goal that has escaped him is playing for an NBA champion. This year may change that, for with Alcindor to worry about rebounds and defense, Robertson could realize his dream. At 32—and despite Cousy's opinion—he still can shoot, pass, run, playmake and control the ball better than anyone else in the pros. Deadly in one-on-one situations, he will back in on his man, turn around and shoot his jump shot right in the defender's eyes. If he wants to shoot, he can score big, as his history proves, and he can get any shot he wants at any time.

That's the ballplayer Milwaukee has landed, and Larry Costello will be delighted to coach him for the Bucks. "Robertson will fit in just perfectly with Alcindor," Costello said when the trade was announced. "He's going to take some of the pressure off Lew." The logic behind that remark can be found in Red Auerbach's appraisal of Robertson, when he compared the Big O to Cousy. "You could guard Cousy with one man," Auerbach said. "You can't guard Oscar with one. It may take three." Not while they're sagging off on Alcindor.

In any poll to determine the best pro five in NBA history, Oscar's name would have to be engraved at one guard position. It was in just such a poll of over 100 coaches to determine the all-time collegiate basketball players that Robertson's name popped up. Way up. The poll-taker, Dave Sendler, found that Big O drew the largest number of votes. "Robertson," wrote Sendler, "naturally got recognition as an unstoppable one-on-one player . . . Coach [John] Wooden [of UCLA], though, remembers Oscar as an assist man: "He was the greatest because he looked for the pass first. Most others look for the shot. He was a team man and he got his points, too."

The words—and the ranking—apply equally to the Oscar Robertson of today. Cincinnati's loss has made Milwaukee a gilt-edged title threat because they now boast the best Mr. Inside *and* the best Mr. Outside in Alcindor and Robertson. This season could provide the crowning touch to the already incomparable career of Oscar Robertson.

WES UNSELD

The basketball career of the Baltimore Bullets' center started when a fifth-grade teacher showed him there was more to school than books. It was hardly an auspicious beginning, and nobody who saw it would have predicted anything like a pro career for little Wes Unseld. As he tells the story, "I was walking past the playground one winter afternoon when the fifth-grade teacher, Mrs. Dickerson, grabbed me. She said we were playing the sixth-grade team and that she needed a replacement for the center, who didn't show up. So she forced me to play. Well, I was just awful. I was clumsy and unsure of myself. I couldn't dribble the ball at all. I was so disgusted with myself that I didn't pick up a basketball again for four years."

Mrs. Dickerson should have been in the stands for the seven-game playoff series between the Bullets and the New York Knickerbockers last year. She would have been proud of "little" Wes, who now packs 240 pounds on a granite-hard 6'7" body. And she would undoubtedly give him an A-plus for the way he learned to play the game she had to drag him into many seasons ago. Even though Baltimore lost the hard-fought series to New York—after coming back to tie it at three games apiece, following the loss of the first two contests—Unseld deserves the lion's share of credit for keeping the Bullets alive for so long. In the seven games he was a bear on both the offensive and defensive boards in a succession of bitter battles with 1970's MVP, Willis Reed. When the smoke had cleared, Wes showed a total of 165 rebounds for the series to Willis' 124, making Unseld's per-game breakdown a resounding 23.5. His most impressive showing came in the third game, won by Baltimore, 127-113. He didn't outrebound just Reed, his 34 retrieves topped the entire Knick total of 30. Along with dominating the New Yorkers off the boards, he whipped in 23 points and added four assists.

Unseld was pleased with his effort but he played down the praise being heaped on him. "That's my job, rebounding," he said in the Bullets dressing room, acknowledging that it was the highest number of rebounds he had ever gotten in a game since entering the NBA. "I didn't do anything different than in the first two games. I was just more successful in blocking out, at getting between my man and the ball."

That man, Willis Reed, doesn't willingly let anyone get between himself and the ball. And he found lots of good things to say about Unseld's powerhouse performance. "I had four fouls and it restricted me some," Reed said. "But it didn't help him get the rebounds. He just did the job. It was a great effort on his part. I've never seen one man outrebound a team before—in the pros, at college or on the playgrounds."

It was indeed a mighty effort, considering that Unseld had placed second in the season's rebound race with a 16.7 per-game average. In many of the 82 games he played in the regular schedule he had an easier time going to the boards than he did in besting a combination like Reed and Dave DeBusschere in the playoffs.

Yet Baltimore coach Gene Shue almost refused to select Unseld as a potential Bullet after seeing him play for the University of Louisville at the 1968 Holiday Festival

Tournament in New York's Madison Square Garden. It wasn't that Unseld played below par, he rebounded strongly, passed off quickly and scored well. It was just that Shue felt, "Unseld's an odd size and awful small to play pivot. His speed is horrible, but he has real good quickness. His shooting must also be considered questionable."

Fortunately for Shue and the Bullets—and unfortunately for the American Basketball Association—the Baltimore coach took a second look at Unseld and decided to take a chance on him. That decision turned into a stroke of genius as Unseld finished his freshman pro season as Rookie of the Year, Player of the Year, the NBA's All-Pro center, and the major reason for Baltimore's leading the Eastern Division after completing the previous season in last place. Shue must have shuddered at the possibility that he might have said "No" to drafting the "odd-sized" center who became the first rookie to be named MVP since Wilt Chamberlain was accorded that honor in 1960.

He also would have missed out on getting a man who adds more than court greatness to a team. Because Wes Unseld is an intelligent, unselfish person for whom admiration extends far beyond the limits of basketball arenas. Success has not spoiled him, even though he's a two-time All-America and often in the spotlight as the heart of the Bullets. Jim Henneman, publicity man for the team, refers to Wes as "a beautiful guy. You know, we often get thank-you notes when one of our players makes an appearance. But you should see the letters we got after Westley had made a number of appearances at playgrounds and clinics in the Baltimore area. He really made an impression. He said he loved to meet people, and they really like him. The best way I can describe him is 'another Brooks Robinson.' And you know what that means in this town."

Author George Vecsey followed Unseld's progress in his rookie season and saw him accept Shue's verdict that he play forward while Leroy Ellis played center. It didn't work out because Ellis wasn't strong enough, and Unseld was moved into the pivot. Vecsey witnessed the birth of a star and expressed his admiration for the unselfishness of Unseld as well as for his playing ability. "It was important," Vecsey wrote of the Ellis-Unseld switch, "because

Westley would throw his thick body in the path of the defenders, setting up screens and picks that Ellis never could have provided. And when the ball zipped in to Westley in the pivot, quite often it zipped right out to somebody with a good, short shot at the basket. Westley, you see, wasn't out for his own points."

Which is why, along with his 13.8 points-per-game mark and 1,491 rebounds, Unseld also notched 213 assists his first year. This brought the following accolade from San Francisco's Jeff Mullins: "Unseld is so unselfish that all he cares about is getting the ball off the board and passing it out to one of his teammates. It's awfully tough to be a selfish player yourself when you've got someone that unselfish on the team with you." To which Atlanta coach Richie Guerin added the final word: "Unseld was the big difference. They were losers before and they're winners now. And Unseld is the only change they made."

Born and raised in Louisville, Kentucky, Wes is one of seven children who grew up with healthy attitudes toward life thanks to their parents. Honesty was held in high regard in the Unseld home. Hard work was another model the elder Unselds gave their children. Mrs. Unseld worked as manager of the grade-school cafeteria young Wes attended, and his father put in many hours at his factory job so that his children could attend college and become respectable citizens. The Baltimore star paid tribute to this parental devotion by saying, "My father worked two jobs to put my two sisters through school at almost the same time. He got himself a couple of heart attacks, but he made sure we got through. My father really sacrificed for us. He's a pretty good old man."

And a pretty good young man is 24-year-old Wes. It didn't take Gene Shue long to learn that, once he stopped experimenting with where and how he was going to play Wes. Not long after installing him permanently as center, Shue said of Unseld, "Actually it's hard to regard him as a rookie. He does the job of a player who's been in the league for years. He's proved to me what his college coach, John Dromo, said is true: that Westley has a keen mind for the game. We found out right away that was true." A few games later, Shue tacked on these thoughts: "He can turn in mid-air and pitch out to one of our guys. I think he's the best man in the league at making a pitchout off the defensive board, even better than Jerry Lucas." And by season's end, he was sky-high in enthusiasm for his rookie center. As Shue described Wes after one playoff game against the Knicks: "He played real good defense, hustled everywhere, showed that he could bring the ball down the court, showed he could hit from the outside, drive, and be a tremendous rebounder. Westley is a complete ballplayer."

Unseld's former teammate, Ray Scott, also speaks of Unseld with such words as "beautiful" and "unselfish." "Wes is just beautiful," Scott said. "The other team shoots, Wes goes for the ball, and the rest of us go charging downcourt. He hits one of our guards at midcourt with one of those two-handed, over-the-head tosses of his and somebody else winds up with an easy layup."

These are the credentials superstar Westley Unseld brings with him as he tries again this year to carry the Bullets past the Knicks and everybody else in a drive for the NBA title. The way the other teams have improved, it will be a rougher road than ever, but don't ever count out any team that lists Wes Unseld at center. He's the guy Gene Shue now refers to as "simply a winning player."

JERRY WEST

If there weren't a basketball player like Jerry West, the NBA would invent one. And how do you invent a Jerry West? Why, you take a man with two special eyes, eyes that work perfectly in making a basketball connect with a hoop when that man tosses the ball at the basket from any angle. Then you add courage, the kind that compels a man to play with pulled muscles, broken bones, with hardly a calorie of energy left in his body. And you pour in equal doses of spirit, determination and unselfish dedication. The result is Jerry West, the Los Angeles Laker described by ex-Celtic Larry Siegfried as "the master. They can talk about the others, build them up, but he is the one. He is the only guard."

And no matter how many times West proves how great he is, he goes himself one better, as if to say, "You ain't seen nothin' yet." Take the third game of the 1970 championship playoffs, Lakers against the N.Y. Knicks. The Knicks score to take a two-point lead with two seconds left in the game. L.A. snaps the ball into play and, with certain defeat two clock-ticks away, the pass reaches West in backcourt. Still 60 feet from the basket, Jerry flicks those special eyes at the hoop and lets fly. At the other end of the court, the ball spins through the circular piece of metal hung from the backboard and rips through the netting. The buzzer goes off but not a soul can hear it as the bellow of surprise and glee of the Forum crowd threatens to deafen everyone in the arena. You had to see it to believe it ... and even then, it was like something out of an incredible script screenwriters stopped dreaming years ago.

In another script, written by Bill Libby, Jerry is described this way: "There may have been or may be better players, though there can not have been many. There may be bigger, stronger, faster, possibly even more skilled players, but it is doubtful anyone has ever played this game harder. West starts, stops, runs again, dribbles, passes, takes a pass, cuts, jumps, shoots, blocks a shot, hounds his man, steals the ball at both ends of the court with every ounce of energy in his skinny body for every second of the 40 or more minutes he plays out of the 48 minutes in every pro game."

Others, not so reluctant to go all out in West's appraisal, say what Bill Sharman did: "He's the greatest player at both ends of the court the game has ever seen."

The ten years Jerry has dedicated to the NBA justify Sharman's statement. In a decade of going against the finest basketball players in the world, Jerry shows a total of 19,144 points scored in regular season play. That breaks down to a per-game average of 27.9 points scored. Yet not until last year did Jerry finally achieve one of the goals he's been chasing since he joined the pros—winning the scoring race. He reached that for the 1969-70 season with a total of 2,309 points and a 31.2 points-per-game average. But you don't earn the distinction of "greatest player at both ends of the court" on scoring alone. Jerry is also one of the leading assist-makers of all time. Last year he finished fourth in the assists derby, handing off for baskets 554 times for a 7.5 per-game average. It was the highest number of assists he has ever collected in one year (his previous top was 480 for 1965-66), which makes his scoring figures even more impressive. His career average for assists now stands at 5.8 per game.

Last season Jerry also kept intact his personal record of picking up the kinds of injury that drive players to the bench. So even though 1969-70 was relatively tame compared to most others in his ten years as a Laker, West still missed 8 games of the schedule. Which fits right in with his medical record that shows up this way in games played per season, starting with 1960-61: 79, 75, 56, 72, 74, 79, 66, 51 and 61. Not only does his nose zig-zag the way he moves on a fast break, his entire body has sustained more breaks, abrasions and tears than the survivors who dared Niagara Falls in a barrel.

At 6-3, 185 pounds, Jerry takes a lot of brutal punishment around the league, especially since he invites it with the driving game he plays. But it's an old story for the 31-year-old superstar who used the same go-go tactics during his high school days at East Bank High, in West Virginia, and continued with more of the same at the University of West Virginia. His college play led to his team's gaining three successive Southern Conference championships, and brought Jerry three designations as All-America. In a recent poll conducted by Dave Sendler for *Sport* Magazine, Jerry was selected by a consensus of 110 college coaches as one of the starting guards on the all-time college team. Looking back on the young Jerry West, coach Frank McGuire of South Carolina described a player who could easily be taken for the Jerry West of today: "Jerry had played a game one night," recalled McGuire, "in which he scored 26 points. But he felt he had not done as well as he should have. He was in the gym the next morning at ten to practice shooting for an hour or so—all alone. That night he went out and scored 36. Another time I saw him break his nose in a game against Kentucky. He went to the sideline to get it packed and then went right back to work. He got 26 points in that game."

That is the West style. He burns up more energy, pours in more points, breaks more bones, wins more games— and insists his teammates deserve the credit. Last year he starred in the All-Star game, made the NBA's All-Star team for the ninth time, was named to the All-Defensive team, and garnered top scoring honors. Yet he says of himself, "I never thought I'd be a big star. And whatever I am, I still don't want to kid myself. I'm not a very good ballhandler or a real good dribbler. I could pass better and defend better. I kick the ball away too often. There are things I practice on. The big guys are the most important men in the game. They control the game at the basket. But the guards are quarterbacks. They set things up. I have to be a good all-around guard as well as a shooter."

But as much as Jerry is his own worst public-relations man—with words—his actions tell the real story. And the men of the NBA aren't shy in their praise of the Kid from Cabin Creek, W. Va. He scores 34 or 35 points in a game and the opposing coach actually smiles and says, "It was a good night for us. Any night you hold West under 40, your defense did its job." Said former Celtic Sam Jones, "He's the greatest I have ever played against." And writer Jim Murray enthused, "There is no more exciting sight in the world of sports than Jerry West dervish-ing down-court with a basketball, eyes and nose flaring, basketball thumping. His shots are a blur."

And while Jerry can never find the words to describe himself as one of the two greatest backcourt men in NBA history, along with Oscar Robertson, he did express his feeling about the game, how it should be played, and how it *shouldn't* be played by athletes drawing big salaries. "I've never been one to take defeat lightly," he told author Bill Libby. "I know it's a cliché to say you hate to lose and I know athletes who say it, but I've also known many athletes on every level, from high school through pro, who couldn't care less, and some who don't even care what they themselves do . . . I hate guys who don't hate to lose, who put themselves ahead of the team, or put themselves ahead of the game. I just don't know how to be that way. I'd really hate like heck to score only one or two baskets in a game, but if we won I'd feel a lot better than if I scored 10 or 20 baskets and we lost, and that's the truth. Basketball is one of the team games and you have to put yourself behind the team.

"I'm a shooter and it's always been my job to shoot, but when it wasn't the right time, I just didn't do it. And if I needed two points to wind up with 20,000 points on the last night of my career, and a shot at that point might cost my team the game, I just wouldn't take the shot, and I mean that. I might feel bad the rest of my life that I didn't get the 20,000, but I'd feel good that I had known it wasn't right to go for it."

As Jerry comes driving out of backcourt this season, one of the marks he'll be gunning for is the exclusive 20,000-points-scored in a career. With less than a thousand to go, it's impossible to imagine he won't have it in his personal record book by mid-season. But when he does that and finishes the 1970-71 season, there's a fair chance that Jerry will retire.

If he does, it will signal the end of another shining era in basketball history—the finish of the Golden Trio: West, Chamberlain and Baylor. For with Wilt and Elgin, the Los Angeles Lakers fielded one of the most awesome offensive fives the game has ever seen. And, many contend, it was West who was the most impressive of all. For if the Lakers were to be beaten, West was the one to stop. Proof of that was plentiful in the 1969-70 season, when, with Chamberlain and Baylor sidelined by injuries, L.A. continued to fight and win games on the strength of one man alone, Jerry West. He did it consistently, playing until he was exhausted, playing with injuries that should have kept him on the bench, too—and playing so well that he inspired the remaining Lakers to hold onto second place until Baylor, and then Chamberlain, could get back in the lineup in time for the playoffs that saw L.A. battle the Knicks for the league championship. It was another typical chapter in the book of Jerry West, described by a teammate in these glowing terms: "He did it for us again. It's a tremendous lift when a player is injured like Jerry was and you know he's possibly endangering himself by playing again. It's a moral lift for you. If he can put out under those conditions, so should everyone else."

And with West as their example, they did. It would have been a sin in the book of Jerry West if they hadn't.

THE PRO OFFENSES

The offenses in professional basketball are strikingly simple compared to those in pro football. Basically, the coaches around the NBA and ABA have the same idea. They each have specialists on their teams who do certain things especially well, and these specialties are what the coaches try to take advantage of. Since pro basketball is, first of all, a running game, the coaches try to have their teams run as much as possible—beat the other team to the basket, get down there before the opposition can get back on defense. When this doesn't work, and it doesn't when a team gets tired, then set plays are set in motion.

These set plays involve "picking" off an opponent; that is, blocking him out to allow the man he is guarding to get free for a shot. The "pick" also forces opponents to switch defensive assignments, the idea being to get a weak or smaller defender on a good and/or taller shooter. The size mismatch occurs when a small man must cover a big man in close to the basket, and the big man's height allows him to shoot with greater ease over the smaller man. A mismatch also occurs when a big man has to guard a smaller and quicker man who has room to maneuver past the big man for an easy shot or drive. If a great shooter—and they come in all sizes in professional basketball (for example: Dave Bing is 6-3, while Mel Counts is 7)—gets even a foot of daylight around the basket, he's going to score at least 50 percent of the time. In fact, if given room, most NBA players can hit close to 40 percent of their shots from any spot on the court. So plays are designed to give them room to shoot, as the following diagrams show:

STANDARD OUT OF BOUNDS
PASS-IN AND SHOT STRATEGY

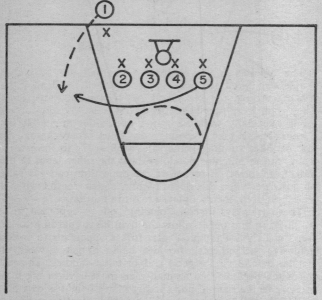

Nos. 2, 3, 4 and 5 line up in a close formation. Then the fastest player, in the No. 5 position, cuts in back of his "blocking line," takes pass-in and gets off a quick, close-in shot.

KEY: Solid line—path of player
Broken line—pass

"CUTBACK" DECOY

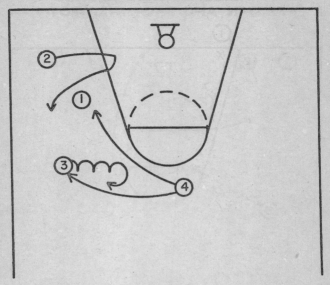

No. 4 passes to No. 3. Then No. 4 drives across the lane to establish a low-post double-screen while No. 3 keeps on dribbling. While No. 3 is moving with the ball, No. 2 weaves out of the corner, heading first toward the basket but then cutting back quickly around the double-screen to take the pass from No. 3. No. 2 is now screened for a short jumpshot.

> **KEY:** Solid line—path of player
> Broken line—pass
> Wavy line—dribble

PHOENIX SUNS' "RIGHT SIDE OPENER"

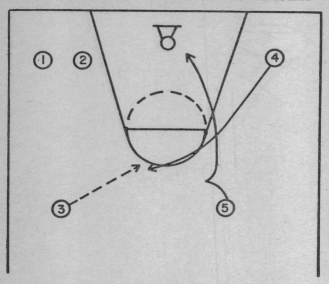

Nos. 1 and 2 clear the lane, leaving a lot of room on the right side. No. 3 hits No. 4 with pass, then No. 4 feeds No. 5, breaking through open area to the basket for layup or short jumpshot.

KEY: Solid line—path of player
Broken line—pass

MILWAUKEE'S "DOUBLE" OPTION

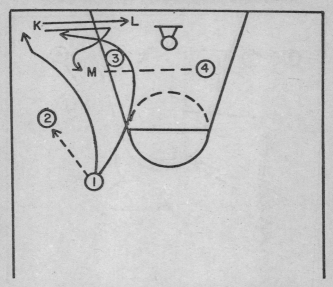

No. 1 passes to No. 2 and continues by path a or b to point k, in the corner. If No. 1 takes path a, and is able to lose his defender on No. 3, he may be free to move to point l for a pass and lay-up. If No. 1 doesn't lose his defender, he can cut back to point m for a jumpshot or pass in to a penetrating teammate, No. 4.

KEY: Solid line—path of player
Broken line—pass

KNICKS' "FREE-FORM" OFFENSE

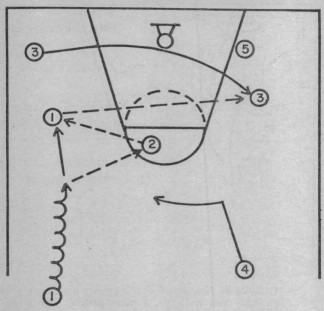

No. 1 dribbles across midcourt line, passes to No. 2 and continues ahead. At the same time, No. 3 crosses to pick up coverage from No. 5. No. 2 then passes back to No. 1 while No. 4 pulls defenseman away from No. 3's area. No. 3 is clear for shot as No. 1 passes to him.

KEY: Solid line—path of player
Broken line—pass
Wavy line—dribble

FINAL STANDINGS & TEAM STATISTICS

	NY	Mil	Balt	Phil	Cinc	Bos	Det	Atl	LA	Chi	Pho	Sea	SF	SD	W	L	Pct	SCORING For	Agst
EAST DIV.																			
New York ———	—	4	5	5	5	3	6	4	4	6	6	4	5	6	60	22	.732	9427	8682
Milwaukee ———	2	—	5	5	4	6	6	2	3	4	5	2	5	5	56	26	.683	9741	9363
Baltimore ———	1	3	—	4	3	5	5	2	2	3	5	5	4	6	50	32	.610	9900	9726
Philadelphia —	2	1	4	—	4	5	4	2	2	3	4	2	3	6	42	40	.512	9998	9718
Cincinnati ——	1	4	3	4	—	5	5	3	2	2	5	3	3	5	36	46	.439	9616	9858
Boston ———	3	2	3	3	1	—	4	2	3	4	3	1	4	3	34	48	.415	9422	9574
Detroit ———	1	0	2	3	2	3	—	3	3	3	3	1	2	4	31	51	.378	9246	9518
WEST DIV.																			
Atlanta ———	4	2	2	2	3	4	3	—	4	5	4	4	5	5	48	34	.585	9646	9612
Los Angeles —	2	3	2	2	2	3	3	2	—	4	4	6	5	5	46	36	.561	9327	9164
Chicago ———	1	2	3	3	2	2	3	1	2	—	5	2	5	6	39	43	.476	9423	9567
Phoenix ———	2	1	1	2	1	3	3	2	2	1	—	3	5	6	39	43	.476	9786	9927
Seattle ———	2	4	1	4	3	5	5	2	0	4	3	—	4	6	36	46	.439	9589	9796
San Francisco	1	1	2	3	3	2	4	1	1	1	1	4	—	5	30	52	.366	9114	9476
San Diego ——	1	1	0	0	1	3	2	1	1	0	1	2	3	—	27	55	.329	9732	9986

TEAM STATISTICS

	G	FIELD GOALS Made	Att.	Pct.	FREE THROWS Made	Att.	Pct.	MISCELLANEOUS Rbds.	Asst.	P.F.	D*	SCORING AVERAGES For	Agst.	Dif.
New York ———	82	3803	7975	.477	1821	2484	.733	4006	2135	2016	10	115.0	105.9	9.1
Milwaukee ———	82	3923	8041	.488	1895	2589	.732	4419	2168	1971	27	118.8	114.2	4.6
Philadelphia —	82	3915	8345	.469	2168	2884	.752	4463	2127	2196	47	121.9	118.5	3.4
Baltimore ———	82	3925	8567	.458	2050	2652	.773	4679	1881	1896	21	120.7	118.6	2.1
Los Angeles —	82	3668	7952	.461	1991	2641	.754	4154	2030	1896	24	113.7	111.8	1.9
Atlanta ———	82	3817	7907	.483	2012	2669	.754	4210	2142	2016	29	117.6	117.2	0.4
Phoenix ———	82	3676	7856	.468	2434	3270	.744	4183	2076	2076	33	119.3	121.1	—1.8
Chicago ———	82	3607	8133	.444	2209	2861	.772	4383	2133	2183	13	114.9	116.7	—1.8
Boston ———	82	3645	8235	.443	2132	2711	.786	4336	1875	2320	41	114.9	116.8	—1.9
Seattle ———	82	3709	8029	.462	2171	2851	.761	4312	2214	2175	42	116.9	119.5	—2.6
Cincinnati ——	82	3767	8271	.455	2082	2841	.733	4163	1992	2215	52	117.3	120.2	—2.9
San Diego ——	82	3866	8867	.436	2000	2728	.733	4786	2036	2096	17	118.7	121.8	—3.1
Detroit ———	82	3565	7657	.466	2116	2881	.734	3831	1709	1930	22	112.8	116.1	—3.3
San Francisco	82	3555	8224	.432	2004	2646	.757	4772	1861	2050	32	111.1	115.6	—4.5

*—Number of games disqualified on personal fouls.

*—Number of games disqualified on personal fouls.
DIVISIONAL SEMI-FINAL SERIES
EASTERN DIVISION
Milwaukee Defeated Philadelphia 4 games to 1
Wed Mar 25 Philadelphia 118, Milwaukee 125 (at Milwaukee)
Fri Mar 27 Philadelphia 112, Milwaukee 105 (at Milwaukee)
Mon Mar 30 Milwaukee 156, Philadelphia 120 (at Philadelphia)
Wed Apr 1 Milwaukee 118, Philadelphia 111 (at Philadelphia)
Fri Apr 3 Philadelphia 106, Milwaukee 115 (at Milwaukee)
New York Defeated Baltimore 4 games to 3
Thu Mar 26 Baltimore 117, New York 120 (2 OT's) (at New York)
Fri Mar 27 New York 106, Baltimore 99 (at Baltimore)
Sun Mar 29 Baltimore 127, New York 113 (at New York)
Tue Mar 31 New York 92, Baltimore 102 (at Baltimore)
Thu Apr 2 Baltimore 80, New York 101 (at New York)
Sun Apr 5 New York 87, Baltimore 96 (at Baltimore)
Mon Apr 6 Baltimore 114, New York 127 (at New York)
DIVISIONAL FINAL SERIES
New York Defeated Milwaukee 4 games to 1
Sat Apr 11 Milwaukee 102, New York 110 (at New York)
Mon Apr 13 Milwaukee 111, New York 112 (at New York)
Fri Apr 17 New York 96, Milwaukee 105 (at Milwaukee)
Sun Apr 19 New York 117, Milwaukee 105 (at Milwaukee)
Mon Apr 20 Milwaukee 96, New York 132 (at New York)
WESTERN DIVISION
Atlanta Defeated Chicago 4 games to 1
Wed Mar 25 Chicago 111, Atlanta 129 (at Atlanta)
Sat Mar 28 Chicago 104, Atlanta 124 (at Atlanta)
Tue Mar 31 Atlanta 106, Chicago 101 (at Chicago)
Fri Apr 3 Atlanta 120, Chicago 131 (at Chicago)
Sun Apr 5 Chicago 107, Atlanta 113 (at Atlanta)
Los Angeles Defeated Phoenix 4 games to 3
Wed Mar 25 Phoenix 112, Los Angeles 128 (at Los Angeles)
Sun Mar 29 Phoenix 114, Los Angeles 101 (at Los Angeles)
Thu Apr 2 Los Angeles 98, Phoenix 112 (at Phoenix)
Sat Apr 4 Los Angeles 102, Phoenix 112 (at Phoenix)
Sun Apr 5 Phoenix 121, Los Angeles 138 (at Los Angeles)
Tue Apr 7 Los Angeles 104, Phoenix 93 (at Phoenix)
Thu Apr 9 Phoenix 94, Los Angeles 129 (at Los Angeles)
Los Angeles Defeated Atlanta 4 games to 0
Sun Apr 12 Los Angeles 119, Atlanta 115 (at Atlanta)
Tue Apr 14 Los Angeles 105, Atlanta 94 (at Atlanta)
Thu Apr 16 Atlanta 114, Los Angeles 115 (OT) (at Los Angeles)
Sun Apr 19 Atlanta 114, Los Angeles 133 (at Los Angeles)
CHAMPIONSHIP SERIES
New York Defeated Los Angeles 4 games to 3
Fri Apr 24 Los Angeles 112, New York 124 (at New York)
Mon Apr 27 Los Angeles 105, New York 103 (at New York)
Wed Apr 29 New York 111, Los Angeles 108 (OT) (at Los Angeles)
Fri May 1 New York 115, Los Angeles 121 (OT) (at Los Angeles)
Mon May 4 Los Angeles 100, New York 107 (at New York)
Wed May 6 New York 113, Los Angeles 135 (at Los Angeles)
Fri May 8 Los Angeles 99, New York 113 (at New York)
1970 NBA CHAMPIONSHIP PLAYOFF FINAL

LOS ANGELES (99)	FG	FT	PTS	NEW YORK (113)	FG	FT	PTS
Baylor	9	1- 2	19	Bradley	8	1- 1	17
Erickson	5	4- 6	14	DeBusschere	8	2- 2	18
Chamberlain	10	1-11	21	Reed	2	0- 0	4
West	9	10-12	28	Barnett	9	3- 3	21
Garrett	3	2- 2	8	Frazier	12	12-12	36
Hairston	2	2- 2	6	Bowman	3	0- 1	6
Tresvant	0	3- 3	3	Riordan	2	1- 2	5
Egan	0	0- 0	0	Russell	1	0- 0	4
Totals	38	23-38	99	Stallworth	1	2- 2	4
				Totals	46	21-23	113

Los Angeles	24	18	27	30— 99
New York	38	31	25	19—113

Fouled out—None. Total fouls—Los Angeles 19, New York 25.
Winning Coach: Red Holzman; Losing Coach: Joe Mullaney.
Attendance: 19,500.

INDIVIDUAL SCORING AVERAGE LEADERS
(Minimum 70 games played)

	G	FG	FT	PTS.	AVG.
J. West, L.A.	74	831	647	2309	31.2
L. Alcindor, Mil.	82	938	485	2361	28.8
E. Hayes, S.D.	82	914	428	2256	27.5
B. Cunningham, Phil.	81	802	510	2114	26.1
L. Hudson, Atl.	80	830	371	2031	25.4
C. Hawkins, Phoe.	81	709	577	1995	24.6
B. Rule, Sea.	80	789	387	1965	24.6
J. Havlicek, Bos.	81	736	488	1960	24.2
E. Monroe, Balt.	82	695	532	1922	23.4
D. Bing, Det.	70	575	454	1604	22.9
T. VanArsdale, Cinc.	71	620	381	1621	22.8
J. Mullins, S.F.	74	656	320	1632	22.1
H. Greer, Phil.	80	705	352	1762	22.0
F. Robinson, Mil.	81	663	437	1765	21.8
W. Reed, N.Y.	81	702	351	1755	21.7
C. Walker, Chi.	78	596	483	1675	21.5
D. VanArsdale, Phoe.	77	592	459	1643	21.3
J. Caldwell, Atl.	82	674	379	1727	21.1
B. Love, Chi.	82	640	442	1722	21.0
J. Walker, Det.	81	666	355	1687	21.0

FIELD GOAL PERCENTAGE LEADERS
(Minimum 700 or more attempts in 70 games)

	G	FG	FGA	PCT.
J. Green, Cinc.	78	481	860	.559
D. Imhoff, Phil.	79	430	796	.540
L. Hudson, Atl.	80	830	1564	.531
J. McGlocklin, Mil.	82	639	1206	.530
D. Snyder, Sea.	82	456	863	.528
J. Fox, Phoe.	81	413	788	.524
L. Alcindor, Mil.	82	938	1810	.518
W. Unseld, Balt.	82	526	1015	.518
W. Frazier, N.Y.	77	600	1158	.518
D. VanArsdale, Phoe.	77	592	1166	.508

FREE THROW PERCENTAGE LEADERS
(Minimum 350 or more attempts in 70 games)

	G	FT	FTA	PCT.
F. Robinson, Mil.	81	439	489	.898
C. Walker, Chi.	78	483	568	.850
J. Mullins, S.F.	74	320	378	.847
J. Havlicek, Bos.	81	488	578	.844
B. Love, Chi.	82	442	525	.842
E. Monroe, Balt.	82	532	641	.830
L. Hudson, Atl.	80	371	450	.824
J. West, L.A.	74	647	785	.824
H. Greer, Phil.	80	352	432	.815
J. Walker, Chi.	81	355	440	.807

LEADERS IN AVERAGE REBOUNDS
(Minimum 70 games or more)

	G	RO.	AVG.
E. Hayes, S.D.	82	1386	16.9
W. Unseld, Balt.	82	1370	16.7
L. Alcindor, Mil.	82	1190	14.5
B. Bridges, Atl.	82	1181	14.4
G. Johnson, Balt.	78	1086	13.9
W. Reed, N.Y.	81	1126	13.9
B. Cunningham, Phil.	81	1101	13.6
T. Boerwinkel, Chi.	81	1016	12.5
P. Silas, Phoe.	78	916	11.7
C. Lee, S.F.	82	929	11.3

LEADERS IN AVERAGE ASSISTS
(Minimum 70 games or more)

	G	NO.	AVG.
L. Wilkens, Sea.	75	683	9.1
W. Frazier, N.Y.	77	629	8.2
C. Haskins, Chi.	82	624	7.6
J. West, L.A.	74	554	7.5
G. Goodrich, Phoe.	81	605	7.5
W. Hazzard, Atl.	82	561	6.8
J. Havlicek, Bos.	81	550	6.8
A. Williams, S.D.	80	503	6.3
N. VanLier, Cinc.	81	500	6.2
D. Bing, Det.	70	418	6.0

Most Points Scored in One Game—L. Hudson, Atl. 57, vs Chi. at Auburn, Ala. 11-10-69

Most Free Throws in One Game—L. Wilkens, Sea., 21, at Philadelphia, 11-8-69
C. Hawkins, Phoe., 21 vs. Seattle, 1-17-70

Most Rebounds in One Game—T. Boerwinkel, Chi., 37, vs. Phoenix, 1-8-70

Most Assists in One Game—A. Williams, S.D., 22, vs San Francisco, 2-14-70

Most Personal Fouls—J. Davis, Atlanta, 335

Most Games Disqualified—N. VanLier, Cinc., 18

INDIVIDUAL STATISTICS

ATLANTA

	G	Minutes	FG Made	FG Att.	FG Pct.	FT Made	FT Att.	FT Pct.	Re-bnd	As-sist	Per Fls.	D*	Tot. Pts.	Avg. Pts.
L. Hudson	80	3091	830	1564	.531	371	450	.824	373	276	225	3	2031	25.4
J. Caldwell	82	2857	674	1329	.507	379	551	.688	407	287	255	1	1727	21.1
W. Hazzard	82	2757	493	1056	.467	267	330	.809	329	561	264	3	1253	15.3
B. Bridges	82	3269	443	932	.475	331	451	.734	1181	345	292	6	1217	14.8
J. Davis	82	2623	438	943	.464	240	318	.755	796	238	335	5	1116	13.6
W. Bellamy***	79	2028	351	671	.523	215	373	.576	707	143	260	5	917	11.6
W. Bellamy**	23	855	141	287	.491	75	124	.605	310	88	97	2	357	15.5
A. Gregor	81	1603	286	661	.433	88	113	.779	397	63	159	5	660	8.1
A. Beard	72	941	183	392	.467	135	163	.828	140	121	124	0	501	7.0
D. Ohl	66	984	176	372	.473	58	72	.806	71	98	113	1	410	6.2
D. Newmark	64	612	127	296	.429	59	77	.766	174	42	128	3	313	4.9
G. O'Malley	24	113	21	60	.350	0	19	.000	26	10	12	0	50	2.1
G. Tormohlen	2	11	2	4	.500	0	0		4	1	3	0	4	2.0
R. Guerin	8	64	3	11	.273	1	1	1.000	2	12	9	0	7	0.9

BALTIMORE

	G	Minutes	FG Made	FG Att.	FG Pct.	FT Made	FT Att.	FT Pct.	Re-bnd	As-sist	Per Fls.	D*	Tot. Pts.	Avg. Pts.
E. Monroe	82	3051	695	1557	.446	532	641	.830	257	402	258	3	1922	23.4
K. Loughery	55	2037	477	1082	.441	253	298	.849	168	292	183	3	1207	21.9
J. Marin	82	2947	666	1363	.489	286	339	.844	537	217	248	6	1618	19.7
G. Johnson	78	2919	578	1282	.451	197	272	.724	1086	264	269	6	1353	17.3
W. Unseld	82	3234	526	1015	.518	273	428	.638	1370	291	250	2	1325	16.2
E. Miles***	47	1295	238	541	.440	133	175	.760	177	86	107	0	609	13.0
E. Miles**	3	52	7	10	.700	3	5	.600	4	4	8	1	17	5.7
M. Davis	56	1330	260	586	.444	149	192	.776	128	111	174	1	669	12.0
R. Scott	73	1393	257	605	.425	139	173	.803	457	114	147	0	653	8.9
L. Ellis	72	1163	194	414	.469	86	116	.741	376	47	129	0	474	6.6
A. Tucker***	61	819	146	285	.512	70	87	.805	166	38	86	0	362	5.9
A. Tucker**	28	262	49	96	.510	33	42	.786	53	7	34	0	131	4.7
F. Carter	76	1219	157	439	.358	80	116	.690	192	121	137	0	394	5.2
B. Quick	15	67	14	28	.500	12	18	.667	12	3	9	0	40	2.7
E. Manning	29	161	32	66	.485	5	8	.625	35	2	33	0	69	2.4
B. Heaney	14	70	13	24	.542	2	4	.500	4	6	17	0	28	2.0

BOSTON

	G	Min-utes	FG Made	FG Att.	FG Pct.	FT Made	FT Att.	FT Pct.	Re-bnd	As-sist	Per Fls	D*	Tot. Pts.	Avg. Pts.
J. Havlicek	81	3369	736	1585	.464	488	578	.844	635	550	211	1	1960	24.2
D. Nelson	82	2224	461	902	.501	337	435	.775	601	148	238	3	1259	15.4
L. Siegfried	78	2081	382	902	.424	220	257	.856	212	299	187	2	984	12.6
B. Howell	82	2078	399	931	.429	235	308	.763	550	120	261	4	1033	12.6
J. White	60	1328	309	684	.452	111	135	.822	169	145	132	1	729	12.2
T. Sanders	57	1616	246	555	.443	161	183	.880	314	92	199	5	653	11.5
H. Finkel	80	1866	310	683	.454	156	233	.670	613	103	292	13	776	9.7
E. Bryant	71	1617	210	520	.404	135	181	.746	269	231	201	5	555	7.8
S. Kuberski	51	797	130	335	.388	64	92	.696	257	29	87	0	324	6.4
J. Barnes	77	1049	178	434	.410	95	128	.742	350	52	229	4	451	5.9
R. Johnson	65	898	167	361	.411	46	70	.657	208	32	155	3	380	5.8
D. Chaney	63	839	115	320	.359	82	109	.752	152	72	118	0	312	5.0
R. Nieman	6	18	2	5	.400	2	2	1.000	6	2	10	0	6	1.0

CHICAGO

	G	Min-utes	FG Made	FG Att.	FG Pct.	FT Made	FT Att.	FT Pct.	Re-bnd	As-sist	Per Fls	D*	Tot. Pts.	Avg. Pts.
C. Walker	78	2726	596	1249	.477	483	568	.850	604	192	203	1	1675	21.5
B. Love	82	3123	640	1373	.466	442	525	.842	712	148	260	2	1722	21.0
C. Haskins	82	3214	668	1486	.450	332	424	.783	378	624	237	0	1668	20.3
J. Sloan	53	1822	310	737	.421	207	318	.651	372	165	179	3	827	15.6
B. Weiss	82	2544	365	855	.427	213	253	.842	227	474	206	0	943	11.5
T. Boerwinkel	81	2335	348	775	.449	150	226	.664	1016	229	255	4	846	10.4
W. Wesley	72	1407	270	648	.417	145	219	.662	455	68	184	1	685	9.5
A. Tucker	33	557	97	189	.513	37	45	.822	113	31	52	0	231	7.0
S. Halimon	38	517	96	244	.393	49	73	.671	68	69	58	0	241	6.3
B. Kauffman	64	775	94	221	.425	88	123	.715	211	76	117	1	276	4.3
E. Manning***	67	777	119	321	.371	42	56	.750	232	36	122	1	280	4.2
E. Manning**	39	616	87	255	.341	37	48	.771	197	34	89	1	211	5.4
J. Petersen	31	231	33	90	.367	26	39	.667	26	23	22	0	92	3.0
J. Baum	3	13	3	11	.273	0	0	.000	4	0	1	0	6	2.0

CINCINNATI

	G	Min-utes	FG Made	FG Att.	FG Pct.	FT Made	FT Att.	FT Pct.	Re-bnd	As-sist	Per Fls.	D*	Tot. Pts.	Avg. Pts.
O. Robertson	69	2865	647	1267	.511	454	561	.809	422	558	175	1	1748	25.3
T. VanArsdale	71	2544	620	1376	.451	381	492	.774	463	155	247	3	1621	22.8
C. Dierking	76	2448	521	1243	.419	230	306	.752	624	169	275	7	1272	16.7
J. Green	78	2278	481	860	.559	254	429	.592	841	112	268	6	1216	15.6
F. Foster	74	2077	461	1026	.449	176	242	.724	310	107	209	2	1098	14.8
J. Lucas	4	118	18	35	.514	5	7	.714	45	9	5	0	41	10.3
N. VanLier	81	2895	302	749	.403	166	224	.741	409	500	329	18	770	9.5
L. Rackley	66	1256	190	423	.449	124	195	.636	378	56	204	5	504	7.6
H. Gilliam	57	1161	179	441	.406	68	91	.747	215	178	163	6	426	7.5
B. Turner***	72	1170	197	468	.421	123	167	.737	304	43	193	0	517	7.2
B. Turner**	69	1095	188	451	.417	118	157	.752	290	42	187	3	494	7.2
A. Smith	32	453	60	148	.405	52	60	.864	33	45	56	0	172	5.4
J. King***	34	391	53	129	.411	33	41	.805	62	52	47	0	139	4.1
J. King**	31	286	34	83	.410	22	27	.815	46	42	39	1	90	2.9
W. Anderzunas	44	370	65	166	.392	29	46	.630	82	9	47	0	159	3.6
B. Cousy	7	34	1	3	.333	3	3	1.000	5	10	11	0	5	0.7

*Number of games disqualified on personal fouls.
**Team Total
***Combined Player Total

DETROIT

	G	Min-utes	FG Made	FG Att.	FG Pct.	FT Made	FT Att.	FT Pct.	Re-bnd	As-sist	Per Fls.	D*	Tot. Pts.	Avg. Pts.
D. Bing	70	2334	575	1295	.440	454	580	.783	299	418	196	0	1604	22.9
J. Walker	81	2869	666	1394	.478	355	440	.807	242	248	203	4	1687	21.0
E. Miles	44	1243	231	531	.435	130	170	.765	173	82	99	0	592	13.5
O. Moore	81	2523	383	805	.476	194	305	.636	900	104	232	3	960	11.9
T. Dischinger	75	1754	342	650	.526	174	241	.722	369	106	213	5	858	11.4
H. Komives	82	2418	363	878	.413	190	234	.812	193	312	247	2	916	11.2
H. Hairston	15	282	57	103	.553	45	63	.714	88	11	36	0	159	10.6
E. Mueller***	78	2353	300	646	.464	189	263	.719	483	205	192	1	789	10.1
E. Mueller**	74	2284	287	614	.467	185	254	.728	469	199	186	3	759	10.3
W. Bellamy	56	1173	210	384	.547	140	249	.562	397	55	163	3	560	10.0
M. McLemore	73	1421	233	500	.466	119	145	.821	336	83	159	0	585	8.0
S. Mix	18	276	48	100	.480	23	39	.590	64	15	31	0	119	6.6
B. Quick***	34	364	63	139	.453	49	71	.690	75	14	50	0	175	5.1
B. Quick**	19	297	49	111	.441	37	53	.698	63	11	41	1	135	7.1
B. Hewitt***	65	1279	110	298	.369	94	164	.574	356	64	130	0	274	4.2
B. Hewitt**	45	801	85	210	.405	54	63	.603	213	36	91	1	208	4.6
P. Long	25	130	28	62	.452	27	38	.711	11	17	22	0	83	3.3
C. Reynolds	10	44	8	19	.421	5	7	.714	14	12	10	0	21	2.1
T. Workman	2	6	0	1	.000	0	0	.000	0	0	1	0	0	0.0

LOS ANGELES

	G	Min-utes	FG Made	FG Att.	FG Pct.	FT Made	FT Att.	FT Pct.	Re-bnd	As-sist	Per Fls.	D*	Tot. Pts.	Avg. Pts.
J. West	74	3106	831	1673	.497	647	785	.824	338	554	160	3	2309	31.2
W. Chamberlain	12	505	129	227	.568	70	157	.446	221	49	31	1	328	27.3
E. Baylor	54	2213	511	1051	.486	276	357	.773	559	292	132	0	1298	24.0
H. Hairston***	70	2427	483	973	.496	326	413	.789	775	121	230	9	1292	18.5
H. Hairston**	56	2145	426	870	.490	281	350	.803	687	110	194	9	1133	21.0
M. Counts	81	2193	434	1017	.427	156	201	.776	683	160	304	5	1024	12.6
R. Garrett	73	2318	354	816	.434	138	162	.852	235	180	236	7	846	11.6
J. Tresvant***	69	1499	264	595	.444	206	284	.725	425	112	204	4	734	10.6
J. Tresvant**	20	221	47	88	.534	23	35	.657	63	17	40	0	117	5.9
K. Erickson	68	1755	258	563	.458	91	122	.746	304	209	175	3	607	8.9
R. Roberson	74	2005	262	586	.447	120	212	.566	672	92	256	7	644	8.7
W. McCarter	40	861	132	349	.378	43	60	.717	83	93	71	0	307	7.3
J. Egan	72	1627	215	491	.438	99	121	.818	104	216	171	2	529	7.3
B. Hewitt	20	478	88	88	.284	16	31	.516	141	28	39	0	66	3.3
M. Lynn	44	403	44	133	.331	31	48	.646	64	30	87	4	119	2.7

MILWAUKEE

	G	Min-utes	FG Made	FG Att.	FG Pct.	FT Made	FT Att.	FT Pct.	Re-bnd	As-sist	Per Fls.	D*	Tot. Pts.	Avg. Pts.
L. Alcindor	82	3534	938	1810	.518	485	743	.653	1190	337	283	8	2361	28.8
F. Robinson	81	2762	663	1391	.477	439	489	.898	263	449	254	5	1765	21.8
J. McGlocklin	82	2966	639	1206	.530	169	198	.854	252	303	164	0	1447	17.6
B. Dandridge	81	2461	434	895	.485	199	264	.754	625	292	279	1	1067	13.2
G. Smith	82	2368	339	664	.511	125	174	.718	712	156	304	8	803	9.8
L. Chappell	75	1134	243	523	.465	135	211	.640	276	56	127	1	621	8.3
F. Crawford	77	1331	243	506	.480	101	148	.682	184	225	181	1	587	7.6
D. Smith	80	1637	237	546	.434	119	185	.643	603	62	167	2	593	7.4
J. Arthurs	11	86	12	35	.343	11	15	.733	14	17	15	0	35	3.2
G. Rodgers	64	749	68	191	.356	67	90	.744	74	213	73	1	203	3.2
B. Greacen	41	292	44	109	.404	18	28	.643	59	27	49	0	106	2.6
S. Williams	11	44	11	24	.454	5	11	.455	7	3	5	0	27	2.5
D. Cunningham	60	416	52	141	.369	22	33	.667	160	28	70	0	126	2.1

NEW YORK

	G	Min-utes	FG Made	FG Att.	FG Pct.	FT Made	FT Att.	FT Pct.	Re-bnd	As-sist	Per Fls.	D*	Tot. Pts.	Avg. Pts.
W. Reed	81	3089	702	1385	.507	351	464	.756	1126	161	287	2	1755	21.7
W. Frazier	77	3040	600	1158	.518	409	547	.748	465	629	203	1	1609	20.9
D. Barnett	82	2772	494	1039	.475	232	325	.714	221	298	220	0	1220	14.9
D. DeBusschere	79	2627	488	1082	.451	176	256	.688	790	194	244	2	1152	14.6
B. Bradley	67	2098	413	897	.460	145	160	.824	239	268	219	0	971	14.5
C. Russell	78	1563	385	773	.498	124	160	.775	236	135	137	0	894	11.5
D. Stallworth	82	1375	239	557	.429	161	225	.716	323	139	194	2	639	7.8
M. Riordan	81	1677	255	549	.464	114	165	.691	194	201	192	1	624	7.7
B. Hosket	36	235	46	91	.505	26	33	.788	63	17	36	0	118	3.3
N. Bowman	81	744	98	235	.417	41	79	.519	257	46	189	2	237	2.9
D. May	37	238	39	101	.386	18	19	.947	52	17	42	0	96	2.6
J. Warren	44	272	44	108	.407	24	35	.686	40	30	53	0	112	2.5

PHILADELPHIA

	G	Min-utes	FG Made	FG Att.	FG Pct.	FT Made	FT Att.	FT Pct.	Re-bnd	As-sist	Per Fls.	D*	Tot. Pts.	Avg. Pts.
B. Cunningham	81	3194	802	1710	.469	510	700	.729	1101	352	331	15	2114	26.1
H. Greer	80	3024	705	1551	.455	352	432	.815	376	405	300	8	1762	22.0
A. Clark	76	2772	594	1198	.496	311	396	.785	301	380	201	2	1499	19.7
D. Imhoff	79	2474	430	796	.540	215	331	.650	754	211	294	7	1075	13.6
J. Washington	79	2459	401	842	.476	204	273	.747	734	104	262	5	1006	12.7
W. Jones	78	1740	366	851	.430	190	226	.841	173	276	210	2	922	11.8
F. Hetzel	63	757	156	323	.483	71	85	.835	207	44	110	3	383	6.1
M. Goukas	80	1558	189	416	.454	106	149	.711	216	222	201	0	484	6.1
L. Jackson	37	583	71	181	.392	60	81	.741	198	50	80	0	202	5.5
G. Wilson	67	836	118	304	.388	122	172	.709	317	52	145	3	358	5.3
B. Ogden	47	357	82	172	.477	27	39	.692	86	31	62	2	191	4.1
D. Scholz	1	1	1	1	1.000	0	0	.000	0	0	0	0	2	2.0

*Number of games disqualified on personal fouls.
**Team Total
***Combined Player Total

PHOENIX

	G	Min-utes	FG Made	FG Att.	FG Pct.	FT Made	FT Att.	FT Pct.	Re-bnd	As-sist	Per Fls.	D*	Tot. Pts.	Avg. Pts.
C. Hawkins	81	3312	709	1447	.490	577	741	.779	846	391	287	4	1995	24.6
D. VanArsdale	77	2966	592	1166	.508	459	575	.798	264	338	282	5	1643	21.3
G. Goodrich	81	3234	568	1251	.454	488	604	.808	340	605	251	3	1624	20.0
J. Fox	81	2041	413	788	.524	218	283	.770	570	93	261	7	1044	12.9
P. Silas	78	2836	373	804	.464	250	412	.607	916	214	266	1	996	12.8
D. Snyder	6	147	22	45	.489	7	8	.875	15	9	20	5	51	8.5
J. Chambers	79	1139	283	658	.430	91	125	.728	219	54	162	3	657	8.3
N. Walk	82	1394	257	547	.470	155	242	.640	455	80	225	2	669	8.2
A. Harris***	81	1553	285	723	.394	86	134	.642	161	231	220	0	656	8.1
A. Harris**	76	1375	257	650	.395	82	125	.656	142	211	209	0	596	7.8
L. Green	58	700	101	234	.432	41	70	.586	276	17	115	2	243	4.2
S. McKenzie	58	525	81	206	.393	58	73	.795	93	52	67	1	220	3.8
N. Johnson	28	136	20	60	.333	8	12	.667	47	12	38	0	48	1.4

SAN DIEGO

	G	Min-utes	FG Made	FG Att.	FG Pct.	FT Made	FT Att.	FT Pct.	Re-bnd	As-sist	Per Fls.	D*	Tot. Pts.	Avg. Pts.
E. Hayes	82	3665	914	2020	.452	428	622	.688	1386	162	270	5	2256	27.5
D. Kojis	56	1578	338	756	.447	181	241	.751	388	78	135	1	857	15.3
J. Barnett	80	2105	450	998	.451	289	366	.790	305	287	222	3	1189	14.9
J. Block	82	2152	453	1025	.442	283	367	.782	609	137	275	2	1193	14.5
S. Lantz	82	2471	455	1027	.443	278	361	.770	255	287	238	2	1188	14.5
R. Williams	72	1228	251	641	.392	96	122	.787	155	165	124	0	598	8.3
B. Adelman	35	717	96	247	.389	68	91	.747	81	113	90	0	260	7.4
B. Smith	75	1198	242	567	.427	66	96	.688	328	75	119	1	550	7.3
T. Kimball	77	1622	218	508	.429	107	185	.578	621	95	187	1	543	7.1
J. Trapp	70	1025	185	434	.426	72	104	.692	309	49	200	3	442	6.3
A. Williams	80	1545	189	464	.407	88	118	.746	292	503	168	0	466	5.8
P. Riley	36	474	75	180	.417	40	55	.727	57	85	68	0	190	5.3

SAN FRANCISCO

	G	Min-utes	FG Made	FG Att.	FG Pct.	FT Made	FT Att.	FT Pct.	Re-bnd	As-sist	Per Fls.	D*	Tot. Pts.	Avg. Pts.
J. Mullins	74	2861	656	1426	.460	320	378	.847	382	360	240	4	1632	22.1
N. Thurmond	43	1919	341	824	.414	261	346	.754	762	150	110		943	21.9
J. King	3	105	19	46	.413	11	14	.786	16	10	8		49	16.3
J. Ellis	76	2380	501	1223	.410	200	270	.741	594	139	281	13	1202	15.8
J. Lucas***	67	2420	405	799	.507	200	255	.784	951	173	166	2	1010	15.1
J. Lucas**	63	2302	387	764	.507	195	248	.786	906	166	159	2	969	15.4
R. Williams	80	2435	452	1046	.432	277	337	.822	190	424	287	7	1181	14.8
C. Lee	82	2641	362	822	.440	178	300	.593	929	80	263	5	902	11.0
J. Turner	3	75	9	17	.529	5	10	.500	14	1	6		23	7.7
D. Gambee	73	951	185	464	.399	156	186	.839	244	55	172	0	526	7.2
B. Lewis	73	1353	213	557	.382	100	152	.658	157	194	170	0	526	7.2
B. Portman	60	813	177	398	.445	66	85	.776	224	28	77	0	420	7.0
A. Smith***	77	1087	153	416	.368	152	170	.894	82	133	122	0	458	5.9
A. Smith**	45	634	93	268	.347	100	110	.909	49	87	66	0	286	6.4
A. Attles	45	676	78	202	.386	75	113	.664	74	142	103	0	231	5.1
D. Schlueter	63	685	82	167	.491	60	97	.619	231	25	108	0	224	3.6

SEATTLE

	G	Min-utes	FG Made	FG Att.	FG Pct.	FT Made	FT Att.	FT Pct.	Re-bnd	As-sist	Per Fls.	D*	Tot. Pts.	Avg. Pts.
B. Rule	80	2959	789	1705	.463	387	542	.714	825	144	278	6	1965	24.6
L. Wilkens	75	2802	448	1066	.420	438	556	.788	378	683	212	5	1334	17.8
B. Boozer	82	2549	493	1005	.491	263	320	.822	717	110	237	2	1249	15.2
D. Snyder***	82	2437	456	863	.528	169	208	.813	323	342	277	8	1081	13.2
D. Snyder**	76	2290	434	818	.531	162	200	.810	308	333	257	7	1030	13.6
J. Tresvant	49	1278	217	507	.428	183	249	.735	362	95	164	4	617	12.6
T. Meschery	80	2294	394	818	.482	196	248	.790	666	157	317	13	984	12.3
A. Harris	5	178	28	73	.384	4	9	.444	19	20	11	0	60	12.0
L. Allen	81	1817	306	692	.442	182	249	.731	211	342	201	1	794	9.8
E. Clemens	78	1487	270	595	.454	111	140	.793	316	116	188	0	651	8.3
E. Mueller	4	69	13	32	.406	4	9	.444	14	6	6	0	30	7.5
D. Winfield	64	771	138	288	.479	87	116	.750	98	102	95	4	363	5.7
D. Murrey	81	1079	153	343	.446	136	186	.731	357	76	191	0	442	5.5
R. Thorn	19	105	20	45	.444	15	24	.625	16	17	8	0	55	2.9
A. Hairston	3	20	3	8	.375	1	1	1.000	5	6	3	0	7	2.3
J. Kennedy	14	82	3	34	.088	2	2	1.000	20	7	7	0	8	0.6

*Number of games disqualified on personal fouls
**Team Total
***Combined Player Total

1970 NBA PLAYOFF STATISTICS

ATLANTA

	G	Min-utes	FG Made	FG Att.	FG Pct.	FT Made	FT Att.	FT Pct.	Re-bnd	As-sist	Per Fls.	D*	Tot. Pts.	Avg. Pts.
J. Caldwell	9	393	93	198	.470	39	60	.650	45	38	34	1	225	25.0
L. Hudson	9	360	78	187	.417	41	50	.820	40	33	34	2	197	21.9
W. Hazzard	7	255	65	130	.500	20	32	.625	24	54	23	0	150	21.4
W. Bellamy	9	368	59	126	.468	33	46	.717	140	35	32	0	151	16.8
R. Guerin	2	56	13	21	.619	7	7	1.000	8	4	6	0	33	16.5
B. Bridges	9	381	44	110	.400	16	27	.593	154	29	37	0	104	11.6
A. Beard	9	146	31	65	.477	19	26	.731	26	8	19	0	81	9.0
D. Newmark	6	42	15	33	.455	4	4	1.000	12	2	8	0	34	5.7
J. Davis	9	117	14	37	.378	10	17	.588	30	6	24	0	38	4.2
G. Gregor	7	67	6	21	.286	4	6	.667	17	2	14	1	16	2.3

BALTIMORE

	G	Min-utes	FG Made	FG Att.	FG Pct.	FT Made	FT Att.	FT Pct.	Re-bnd	As-sist	Per Fls.	D*	Tot. Pts.	Avg. Pts.
E. Monroe	7	299	74	154	.481	48	60	.800	23	28	23	0	196	28.0
G. Johnson	7	298	51	111	.459	27	34	.794	80	9	20	1	129	18.4
J. Marin	7	265	48	114	.421	29	34	.853	47	22	27	0	125	17.9
F. Carter	7	253	41	107	.383	17	28	.607	31	24	27	1	99	14.1
W. Unseld	7	289	29	70	.414	15	19	.789	165	24	25	0	73	10.4
K. Loughery	7	153	26	77	.338	15	21	.714	16	8	24	0	67	9.6
R. Scott	7	90	11	34	.324	10	14	.714	21	4	5	0	32	4.6
E. Miles	5	63	4	10	.400	0	0	.000	5	0	8	0	8	1.6
A. Tucker	3	5	2	2	1.000	0	0	.000	0	0	0	0	4	0.7
L. Ellis	4	8	0	4	.000	2	2	1.000	3	0	0	0	2	0.0
B. Heaney	6	7	0	2	.000	0	0	.000	1	1	0	0	0	0.0

CHICAGO

	G	Min-utes	FG Made	FG Att.	FG Pct.	FT Made	FT Att.	FT Pct.	Re-bnd	As-sist	Per Fls.	D*	Tot. Pts.	Avg. Pts.
C. Walker	5	178	35	83	.422	27	33	.818	42	11	14	0	97	19.4
T. Boerwinkel	5	177	40	79	.506	8	13	.615	72	16	19	0	88	17.6
C. Haskins	5	154	32	68	.471	17	19	.895	16	25	13	0	81	16.2
J. Sloan	5	190	29	74	.392	16	25	.640	39	11	18	0	74	14.8
B. Love	5	172	20	52	.385	19	24	.792	46	4	12	0	59	11.8
B. Weiss	5	121	25	59	.424	8	10	.800	6	24	11	0	58	11.6
S. Halimon	5	106	21	61	.344	2	3	.667	20	18	13	0	44	8.8
W. Wesley	4	59	16	31	.516	6	12	.500	19	2	9	0	38	7.6
E. Manning	2	29	5	10	.500	1	2	.500	9	3	2	0	11	2.2
B. Kauffman	3	14	1	3	.333	2	3	.667	6	4	2	0	4	1.3

LOS ANGELES

	G	Min-utes	FG Made	FG Att.	FG Pct.	FT Made	FT Att.	FT Pct.	Re-bnd	As-sist	Per Fls.	D*	Tot. Pts.	Avg. Pts.
J. West	11	495	124	258	.481	95	122	.779	42	97	34	1	343	31.2
W. Chamberlain	11	518	88	176	.500	59	135	.437	230	53	24	0	235	21.4
E. Baylor	11	387	86	189	.455	39	54	.722	94	50	28	2	211	19.2
R. Garrett	11	338	64	120	.533	11	14	.786	31	24	44	0	139	12.6
K. Erickson	10	282	37	82	.451	14	17	.824	46	41	23	0	88	8.8
H. Hairston	10	191	31	74	.419	17	24	.708	50	11	19	1	79	7.9
J. Tresvant	7	111	20	42	.476	7	8	.875	27	11	13	2	47	6.7
M. Counts	11	185	32	74	.432	9	10	.900	66	15	41	0	73	6.6
J. Egan	9	90	13	24	.542	5	6	.833	4	16	8	0	31	3.4
R. Roberson	6	51	5	12	.417	5	8	.625	12	0	9	0	15	2.5
M. Lynn	2	5	2	3	.667	0	0	.000	2	1	1	0	4	2.0
W. McCarter	4	12	3	6	.500	1	1	1.000	2	2	2	0	7	1.8

MILWAUKEE

	G	Min-utes	FG Made	FG Att.	FG Pct.	FT Made	FT Att.	FT Pct.	Re-bnd	As-sist	Per Fls.	D*	Tot. Pts.	Avg. Pts.
L. Alcindor	10	435	139	245	.567	74	101	.733	168	41	25	1	352	35.2
B. Dandridge	10	399	72	142	.507	19	29	.655	87	57	39	1	163	16.3
J. McGlocklin	10	377	62	144	.431	25	31	.806	36	21	22	0	149	14.9
F. Robinson	10	300	42	129	.326	44	50	.880	23	50	22	0	128	12.8
G. Smith	10	329	47	94	.500	13	22	.591	85	22	34	1	107	10.7
F. Crawford	10	208	34	88	.386	20	24	.833	35	37	27	1	88	8.8
L. Chappell	9	133	28	50	.560	13	19	.684	26	5	10	0	69	7.7
D. Smith	7	82	11	19	.579	8	10	.800	26	4	5	0	30	4.3
S. Williams	2	16	4	7	.571	0	0	.000	4	1	5	0	8	4.0
D. Cunningham	8	45	10	18	.556	1	2	.500	12	2	6	0	21	2.6
G. Rodgers	7	68	4	14	.286	9	12	.750	4	21	7	0	17	2.4
B. Greacen	1	8	1	4	.250	0	1	.000	2	3	0	0	2	2.0

*Number of games disqualified on personal fouls

NEW YORK

	G	Min-utes	FG Made	FG Att.	FG Pct.	FT Made	FT Att.	FT Pct.	Re-bnd	As-sist	Per Fls.	D*	Tot. Pts.	Avg. Pts.
W. Reed	11	506	119	256	.465	50	61	.820	185	34	45	0	288	24.0
D. Barnett	12	430	79	164	.482	33	44	.750	23	34	33	0	191	15.9
W. Frazier	12	532	72	162	.444	37	49	.755	95	83	32	0	181	15.1
D. DeBusschere	12	434	70	177	.395	32	50	.640	132	28	39	0	172	14.3
B. Bradley	12	367	62	135	.459	26	33	.788	44	41	34	0	150	12.5
C. Russell	12	176	51	106	.481	11	12	.917	22	6	17	0	113	9.4
M. Riordan	12	205	41	86	.526	19	28	.679	33	17	19	0	101	8.4
D. Stallworth	12	177	40	86	.465	8	9	.889	44	9	22	0	88	7.3
B. Hosket	3	20	3	6	.500	3	4	.750	4	1	4	0	9	3.0
D. May	2	7	2	3	.667	0	0	.000	0	0	2	0	4	2.0
N. Bowman	12	60	5	20	.250	4	5	.800	23	4	18	0	14	1.3
J. Warren	6	16	1	4	.250	0	0	.000	3	1	3	0	2	0.3

PHILADELPHIA

	G	Min-utes	FG Made	FG Att.	FG Pct.	FT Made	FT Att.	FT Pct.	Re-bnd	As-sist	Per Fls.	D*	Tot. Pts.	Avg. Pts.
B. Cunningham	5	205	61	123	.496	14	36	.667	52	20	19	0	146	29.2
W. Jones	5	160	34	65	.523	11	14	.786	11	24	16	0	79	15.8
H. Greer	5	178	33	74	.446	11	13	.846	17	27	16	0	77	15.4
A. Clark	5	146	26	60	.433	16	22	.727	14	18	10	0	68	13.6
J. Washington	5	167	25	57	.439	13	23	.565	49	9	18	0	63	12.6
B. Ogden	1	12	5	9	.556	2	4	.500	1	9	0	0	12	12.0
D. Imhoff	5	138	22	48	.458	1	7	.143	35	6	23	0	45	9.0
F. Hetzel	5	75	13	25	.520	9	11	.818	18	11	10	0	35	7.0
M. Goukas	2	23	6	8	.750	1	1	1.000	3	3	1	0	13	6.5
G. Wilson	2	23	4	13	.308	1	1	1.000	12	1	4	0	9	4.5
L. Jackson	5	73	9	19	.474	2	2	1.000	33	3	11	1	20	4.0

PHOENIX

	G	Min-utes	FG Made	FG Att.	FG Pct.	FT Made	FT Att.	FT Pct.	Re-bnd	As-sist	Per Fls.	D*	Tot. Pts.	Avg. Pts.
C. Hawkins	7	328	62	150	.413	54	66	.818	97	41	22	0	178	25.4
G. Goodrich	7	265	56	118	.475	30	35	.857	32	38	21	0	142	20.3
T. VanArsdale	7	255	43	100	.430	29	33	.878	18	29	23	1	115	16.4
P. Silas	7	286	46	109	.330	21	32	.656	111	30	29	0	113	16.1
J. Fox	6	174	25	69	.362	17	24	.708	64	20	20	1	67	11.2
N. Walk	5	63	17	43	.395	6	8	.750	35	8	13	0	40	8.0
J. Chambers	7	73	14	37	.378	5	8	.625	17	2	6	0	33	4.7
A. Harris	7	89	15	42	.357	0	2	.000	13	12	13	0	30	4.3
L. Green	6	69	8	28	.286	2	5	.400	23	5	13	0	18	3.0
S. McKenzie	7	71	8	29	.276	4	5	.800	9	3	14	0	16	2.3
N. Johnson	2	7	1	3	.333	0	0	.000	4	0	4	0	2	1.0

FIRST ALL-STAR TEAM

Player, Team	Vote	Pos.
Billy Cunningham, Philadelphia	13.002	F
Connie Hawkins, Phoenix	7.739	F
Willis Reed, New York	10.113	C
Jerry West, Los Angeles	14.000	G
Walt Frazier, New York	10.598	G

SECOND ALL-STAR TEAM

Player, Team	Vote	Pos.
John Havlicek, Boston	7.360	F
Gus Johnson, Baltimore	3.621	F
Lew Alcindor, Milwaukee	10.094	C
Lou Hudson, Atlanta	6.563	G
Oscar Robertson, Cincinnati	4.154	G

TEAM SHOOTING

2-PT FG	Made	Attempts	Pct.
Indiana	3378	7112	.475
Washington	3601	7636	.472
Dallas	3588	7681	.467
Denver	3555	7697	.462
New York	3473	7572	.459
Pittsburgh	3593	7893	.455
Los Angeles	3444	7631	.451
Carolina	3381	7530	.449
New Orleans	3295	7386	.446
Miami	3510	8003	.439
Kentucky	3263	7455	.438

3-PT FG	Made	Attempts	Pct.
Kentucky	330	923	.358
Dallas	187	584	.320
Washington	108	352	.307
New Orleans	168	596	.282
Denver	188	684	.275
Indiana	215	784	.274
Carolina	89	329	.271
Pittsburgh	128	477	.268
Los Angeles	131	489	.268
Miami	88	342	.257
New York	70	282	.248

FREE THROWS	Made	Attempts	Pct.
Dallas	2340	2968	.788
New Orleans	1970	2531	.778
Washington	2403	3177	.756
Los Angeles	2266	3022	.750
Denver	2023	2713	.746
Miami	2225	2991	.744
Indiana	2110	2846	.741
Kentucky	2020	2733	.739
Carolina	1942	2662	.730
New York	1990	2826	.704
Pittsburgh	1874	2673	.701

AMERICAN BASKETBALL ASSOCIATION STATISTICS

EASTERN	Ind.	Ken.	Car.	N.Y.	Pit.	Mia.	Den.	Dal.	Was.	L.A.	N.O.		Won	Lost	Pct.	GB
Indiana	—	9-2	6-4	6-5	10-1	9-2	4-2	2-4	5-1	4-2	4-2	—	59	25	.702	—
Kentucky	2-9	—	6-5	7-4	6-5	7-3	3-3	4-2	5-1	2-4	4-2	—	45	39	.536	14
Carolina	4-6	5-6	—	7-4	6-5	6-5	1-5	5-1	3-3	1-5	3-3	—	42	42	.500	17
New York	5-6	4-7	4-7	—	7-3	8-3	3-3	2-4	2-4	2-4	2-4	—	39	45	.464	20
Pittsburgh	1-10	5-6	5-6	3-7	—	7-4	2-4	2-4	1-5	1-5	2-4	—	29	55	.345	30
Miami	2-9	3-7	5-6	3-8	4-7	—	1-5	2-4	0-6	2-4	1-5	—	23	61	.274	36
WESTERN													Won	Lost	Pct.	GB
Denver	2-4	3-3	5-1	3-3	4-2	5-1	—	8-4	7-5	9-3	5-7	—	51	33	.607	—
Dallas	4-2	2-4	1-5	4-2	4-2	4-2	4-8	—	7-5	9-3	6-6	—	45	39	.536	6
Washington	1-5	1-5	3-3	4-2	5-1	6-0	5-7	5-7	—	8-4	6-6	—	44	40	.524	7
Los Angeles	2-4	4-2	5-1	4-2	5-1	4-2	3-9	3-9	4-8	—	9-3	—	43	41	.512	8
New Orleans	2-4	4-2	3-3	2-4	4-2	5-1	7-5	6-6	6-6	3-9	—	—	42	42	.500	9

Team	GP	Team TP Offense	Offense Avg.	Team Defense TP	Defense Avg.	Score Diff.	Own Reb.	Opp. Reb.	Reb. Diff.	As-sists	Er-rors	PF Avg.
Denver	84	9697	115.4	9328	111.0	+4.4	57.7	52.9	+4.8	19.3	16.7	24.6
Indiana	84	9511	113.2	9220	109.7	+3.5	52.8	54.4	-1.6	21.7	17.7	25.3
Dallas	84	10079	120.0	9918	118.1	+1.9	55.2	55.4	-0.2	21.0	20.3	25.4
Kentucky	84	9536	113.5	9450	112.5	+1.0	56.4	54.3	+2.1	19.4	19.5	28.7
New Orleans	84	9064	107.9	8999	107.1	+0.8	52.9	53.6	-0.7	21.0	18.2	24.9
Carolina	84	9031	107.5	8990	107.0	+0.5	51.3	52.2	-0.9	19.5	19.3	26.7
Los Angeles	84	9547	113.7	9567	113.9	-0.2	54.7	56.1	-1.4	20.8	19.0	26.6
Washington	84	9929	118.2	9983	118.9	-0.7	55.1	54.6	+0.5	21.1	23.7	27.7
New York	84	9148	108.9	9219	109.8	-0.9	49.5	51.4	-1.9	23.3	20.4	28.3
Miami	84	9511	113.2	9940	118.3	-5.1	53.5	52.3	+1.2	15.3	18.7	27.0
Pittsburgh	84	9445	112.4	9884	117.7	-5.3	56.2	58.0	-1.8	19.4	21.0	26.0

INDIVIDUAL SCORING LEADERS (Minimum 1,200 Points)

No. Player, Club	GP	FG	FT	Pts.	Avg.
1. Spencer Haywood, Denver	84	986	547	2519	29.99
2. Rick Barry, Washington	52	509	400	1442	27.73
3. Bob Verga, Carolina	82	801	458	2258	27.54
4. Don Freeman, Miami	79	761	626	2163	27.38
5. Louie Dampier, Kentucky	82	545	447	2125	25.91
6. Larry Jones, Denver	75	584	579	1870	24.93
7. Levern Tart, New York	80	745	412	1935	24.19
8. Darel Carrier, Kentucky	77	503	454	1781	23.13
9. Roger Brown, Indiana	84	679	457	1935	23.04
10. Glen Combs, Dallas	84	510	458	1868	22.24
11. Steve Jones, New Orleans	84	674	412	1805	21.49
12. John Brisker, Pittsburgh	77	593	329	1617	21.00
13. Don Sidle, Miami	84	638	469	1749	20.82
14. James Jones, New Orleans	70	531	380	1448	20.69
15. Bob Netolicky, Indiana	82	671	343	1691	20.62
16. Cincy Powell, Dallas	76	560	402	1528	20.11
17. Manny Leaks, Dallas	84	636	305	1577	18.77
18. Mel Daniels, Indiana	83	613	330	1556	18.75
19. John Beasley, Dallas	84	623	284	1539	18.32
20. Gene Moore, Kentucky	83	628	209	1471	17.72
21. Doug Moe, Carolina	80	527	304	1382	17.27
22. Mack Calvin, Los Angeles	84	438	529	1414	16.83
23. Les Hunter, New York	79	480	317	1295	16.39
24. Fred Lewis, Indiana	81	401	383	1326	16.37
25. Austin Robbins, New Orleans	82	518	285	1342	16.37

Three-point field goals—Barry 8, Verga 66, Freeman 5, Dampier 198, L. Jones 41, Tart 11, Carrier 105, R. Brown 40, Combs 130, S. Jones 15, Brisker 34, Sidle 1, J. Jones 2, Netolicky 2, Powell 2, J. Beasley 3, Moore 2, Moe 8, Calvin 3, Hunter 6, F. Lewis 47, Robbins 7.

INDIVIDUAL REBOUNDING LEADERS (Minimum 750 Rebounds)

No. Player, Club	GP	Offense	Defense	Rebounds	Avg.
1. Spencer Haywood, Denver	84	533	1104	1637	19.49
2. Mel Daniels, Indiana	83	423	1039	1462	17.61
3. Austin Robbins, New Orleans	82	427	905	1332	16.24
4. Gerald Govan, New Orleans	84	285	932	1217	14.49
5. Ira Harge, Washington	84	334	843	1177	14.01
6. Mike Lewis, Pittsburgh	78	370	684	1054	13.51
7. Jim Ligon, Kentucky	84	399	695	1094	13.02
8. Don Sidle, Miami	84	432	650	1082	12.88
9. Manny Leaks, Dallas	84	427	620	1047	12.46
10. Gene Moore, Kentucky	83	345	657	1002	12.07
11. John Beasley, Dallas	84	303	703	1006	11.98
12. Ed Johnson, New York	74	328	551	879	11.88
13. Willie Wise, Los Angeles	82	283	669	952	11.61
14. Warren Davis, Pittsburgh	80	278	629	907	11.34
15. Bob Netolicky, Indiana	82	337	539	876	10.68

2-PT FIELD GOALS (Minimum 325 Made)

No. Player, Team	Made	Att.	Pct.
1. Frank Card, Washington	350	661	.530
2. Byron Beck, Denver	440	839	.524
3. Arvesta Kelly, Pittsburgh	363	704	.516
4. Roger Brown, Indiana	679	1324	.513
5. Rick Barry, Washington	509	997	.511
6. Gene Littles, Carolina	414	814	.509
7. Jim Ligon, Kentucky	507	998	.508
8. John Beasley, Dallas	623	1246	.500
9. James Jones, New Orleans	531	1063	.500
10. Julian Hammond, Denver	329	659	.499

3-PT FIELD GOALS (Minimum 50 Made)

No. Player, Team	Made	Att.	Pct.
1. Darel Carrier, Kentucky	105	280	.375
2. Louie Dampier, Kentucky	198	548	.361
3. Jeff Congdon, Denver	63	178	.354
4. Glen Combs, Dallas	130	370	.351
5. Mike Barrett, Wash.	62	180	.344
6. George Lehmann, Miami	92	286	.322
7. George Stone, L.A.	65	206	.316
8. Bob Verga, Carolina	66	215	.307
9. Mike Butler, New Orleans	87	300	.290
10. Lonnie Wright, Denver	54	193	.280

FREE THROWS (Minimum 250 Made)

No. Player, Team	Made	Att.	Pct.
1. Darel Carrier, Kentucky	454	509	.892
2. Rick Barry, Washington	400	463	.864
3. Glen Combs, Dallas	458	548	.836
4. Steve Jones, New Orleans	412	495	.832
5. Louie Dampier, Kentucky	447	538	.831
6. John Brisker, Pittsburgh	329	398	.827
7. Larry Brown, Washington	362	439	.825
8. Mack Calvin, Los Angeles	529	642	.824
9. Don Freeman, Miami	626	762	.822
10. Bill Melchionni, New York	255	311	.820

ASSISTS (Minimum 325 Made)

No. Player, Team	GP	No.	Avg.
1. Larry Brown, Washington	82	580	7.07
2. Bill Melchionni, New York	80	457	5.71
3. Mack Calvin, Los Angeles	84	478	5.69
4. Larry Jones, Denver	75	426	5.68
5. Louie Dampier, Kentucky	82	447	5.45
6. Jeff Congdon, Denver	83	446	5.37
7. Doug Moe, Carolina	80	435	5.31
8. James Jones, New Orleans	70	340	4.86
9. Roger Brown, Indiana	84	392	4.67
10. Gerald Govan, New Orleans	84	385	4.58

NBA ALL-STAR TEAM

NEW YORK—Jerry West, completing the best season of his starry 10-year career with the Los Angeles Lakers, was named as the only unanimous player on the 1969-70 National Basketball Association All-Star team.

The squad, selected by a panel of sportswriters and sportscasters in the 14 member cities and announced by Commissioner Walter Kennedy, also contained two members of the New York Knicks.

Center Willis Reed, the Association's Most Valuable Player, and guard Walt Frazier are the first Knicks so honored since Harry Gallatin 16 seasons ago, when New York last won an Eastern Division Championship.

Billy Cunningham of Philadelphia—next to West the top vote-getter on the 24th annual team—joins newcomer Connie Hawkins of Phoenix at forward on the first team.

John Havlicek of Boston and Gus Johnson of Baltimore are the second-team forwards. Lew Alcindor of Milwaukee, the only rookie on either team, is at center, with Atlanta's Lou Hudson and Oscar Robertson, playing for Cincinnati, at guard.

Each franchised city received one full vote in the balloting, making 14.000 a perfect score. West is the first unanimous selection since Wilt Chamberlain, then with the Philadelphia 76ers, in 1968.

For West, it was a gratifying honor because the 6-3 guard was nosed out for first team honors in 1967-68 and 1968-69. This season he led the Association in scoring average with 31.2 points per game, finished second in the Most Valuable Player voting, and recaptured first team All-Star honors. He has been named to the first team seven times and twice to the second team.

It is the first All-Star first-team selections for Hawkins, Reed and Frazier. Reed made second team three times. Cunningham was the leading vote-getter in the All-Star balloting last year when he made first-team status for the first time.

Alcindor and Hudson made second-team honors for the first time. Johnson has been so honored three times and Havlicek four. Robertson missed out on first team honors this season for the first time since turning pro in 1960.

Three men who made first team in 1968-69 missed out completely this season—Elgin Baylor of Los Angeles, Wes Unseld and Earl Monroe of Baltimore.

The closest race for first team this year was at center. Reed compiled a vote of 10.113, while Alcindor finished with 10.094, a difference of just 19/1000s of a point.

NBA ALL-ROOKIE TEAM

Lew Alcindor and Bob Dandridge of the Milwaukee Bucks were the top vote-getters on the National Basketball Association's All-Rookie team for the 1969-70 season as announced by Commissioner Walter Kennedy.

Alcindor was named unanimously in the balloting of NBA coaches. The 7-1½ star center also was named Rookie of the Year unanimously. He was second in the NBA in scoring average with 28.8 and third in rebounds with an average of 14.5 per game. He also led all NBA centers in assists with 337.

Dandridge, a 6-7 forward from Norfolk State and a fourth-round draft pick, scored 13.2 points per game for the young Bucks and was voted to the team by 12 of the 14 coaches.

Completing the All-Rookie team are JoJo White of the Boston Celtics, Dick Garrett, who played for the Los Angeles Lakers but was drafted by the newly formed Buffalo club, and Mike Davis, who played for the Baltimore Bullets but who was traded to Buffalo.

Those who also received more than one vote were Norm Van Lier of Cincinnati, Lucius Allen of Seattle and Rick Roberson of Los Angeles.

Alcindor and Dandridge form the first teammate tandem selected since 1968, when New York placed Walt Frazier and Phil Jackson, and Seattle had Bob Rule and Al Tucker.

White, a product of the University of Kansas, became a starter in Boston's backcourt and averaged 12.2 points per game. Garrett, a 6-3 guard from Southern Illinois, received extensive playing time as a rookie with the Lakers, averaging 11.6 points per game.

Davis averaged 12 points a game for Baltimore before a late-season wrist injury sidelined him.

Votes	NBA All-Rookie Team
14	Lew Alcindor, Milwaukee
12	Bob Dandridge, Milwaukee
8	Jo Jo White, Boston
7	Dick Garrett, Los Angeles
7	Mike Davis, Baltimore

Honorable Mention—Norm Van Lier, Cincinnati; Lucius Allen, Seattle; and Rick Roberson, Los Angeles.

NBA'S ALL-DEFENSIVE TEAM

Walt Frazier, New York's outstanding backcourt star, was the top vote-getter for the second consecutive year for the National Basketball Association's All-Defensive team announced by Commissioner Walter Kennedy and Newspaper Enterprise Association.

Frazier received 27 of a possible 28 points in the second annual balloting of the 14 NBA coaches. Each first team selection receives two points and the second team choices get one point each.

Frazier is by no means New York's only representative on the first team.

The Knicks, who allowed their opponents fewer points per game (105.9) than any other NBA team, placed three men on the first team—Frazier, forward Dave DeBusschere and center Willis Reed.

Gus Johnson of the Baltimore Bullets, who thrilled sellout crowds in New York and Baltimore during the Eastern Division Semi-Final Playoffs with his individual duel with DeBusschere, also made the first team.

Completing the first five is Jerry West of the Los Angeles Lakers, who demonstrated his versatility by leading the Association in scoring average with 31.2 points per game.

On the second All-Defensive team are forwards John Havlicek of Boston and Bill Bridges of Atlanta, center Lew Alcindor of Milwaukee, and guards Joe Caldwell of Atlanta and Jerry Sloan of Chicago.

Frazier and DeBusschere are the only repeaters on the first team from the 1968-69 All-Defensive team, established to honor this highly specialized phase of the game.

"Defense wins games," Frazier said—and his play proves it.

He matches up with the opposing team's stronger-shooting guards, following them step for step and so many times starting the fast-breaking New York offense by gambling—poking at the ball, stealing it and setting up a play.

"I take a lot of pride in defense," Frazier points out. "I work at it. I always watch the ball."

Frazier, a third-year guard from Southern Illinois, scored 20.9 points a game, second on the Knicks behind

Reed, and finished second in the NBA in assists average at 8.2 per game.

Members of the communications media, recognizing his talents on both offense and defense, voted Walt Frazier the starting guard's position for the 1970 All-Star Game at Philadelphia. It was the first such selection for the 25-year-old guard.

DeBusschere was the second-highest vote-getter on the team with 24 points, and West was third with 23.

Havlicek and Bridges also made the second team a year ago.

For Caldwell, the selection was gratifying because he is one of the few players in the NBA switching positions constantly. The springy-legged 6-5 Caldwell is a forward on offense, although he played guard there a year ago so well, he made the All-Star Game lineup.

Defensively this season, Caldwell played guard against most clubs, prompting both West and Frazier to publicly praise him for his defensive exploits against them. Yet he also frustrates certain strong-shooting forwards when Atlanta plays them.

Sloan, Chicago's fine rebounding guard with a widespread reputation for his strong defense, had made the All-Defensive first team last year. He missed 29 games with injuries this season, yet still made the second team.

Alcindor is the first rookie to make the All-Defensive team in its two years. His outstanding play, defensively as well as when Milwaukee had possession, helped the Bucks leapfrog from last place to second in the Eastern Division.

1969-70 NBA ALL-DEFENSIVE TEAM

FIRST TEAM

Player Team	Pos.	Yrs. Pro.	Pts.
Dave DeBusschere, N.Y.	F	8	24
Gus Johnson, Baltimore	F	7	17
Willis Reed, New York	C	6	15
Walt Frazier, New York	G	3	27
Jerry West, Los Angeles	G	10	23

SECOND TEAM

Player Team	Pos.	Yrs. Pro.	Pts.
John Havlicek, Boston	F	8	9
Bill Bridges, Atlanta	F	8	7
Lew Alcindor, Milwaukee	C	1	11
Joe Caldwell, Atlanta	G	6	8
Jerry Sloan, Chicago	G	5	5

JERRY WEST WINS NBA SCORING
AVERAGE CHAMPIONSHIP

NEW YORK—Irrepressible Jerry West, a 10-year National Basketball Association veteran who has scored more than 19,000 points, finally achieved one of the few elusive goals not reached earlier in his starry career—the league's scoring average championship.

West poured in 2,309 points in 74 games for a 31.2 points per game average. He also helped the injury-weakened Lakers finish second in the Western Division.

West finished second to Chamberlain two times in the scoring race. In 1964-65, Jerry averaged 31.0 points per game to Wilt's 34.7. The following year, West was 31.4 (his best scoring season) and Chamberlain finished at 33.5.

But this year West led the league since Nov. 16 and was typically modest in analyzing why he won the scoring title.

"I feel a lot of this has to do with circumstances this year, with Elgin and Wilt hurt so much," he said. "It gave me an opportunity to be a bigger part of our offense.

"It's more gratifying to me that I could do this at 31 years of age, especially since I've had some sort of enigma? about injuries and this year I've been able to avoid them. That is what I'm proud of."

Milwaukee rookie Lew Alcindor finished second to West with a 28.8 average and San Diego's Elvin Hayes, the defending champion, finished third at 27.5.

HAYWOOD, CARRIER EACH WIN 2 TITLES
IN ABA STATISTICAL DEPARTMENTS

Denver's Spencer Haywood and Kentucky's Darel Carrier each won a pair of individual statistical titles during the 1969-70 American Basketball Association regular season. Final statistics rank Haywood first in scoring and rebounding, while Carrier won top honors in shooting percentage on 3-point field goals and free throws. It's the third straight year Carrier has led the league in 3-point field goal percentage.

Washington's Larry Brown captured his third consecutive playmaking crown and teammate Frank Card took the 2-point field goal percentage title with a closing rush in the final two weeks of the season.

Haywood was the big story. He scored the most points (2,519) and had the best scoring average (29.99). He also grabbed the most rebounds (1,637) and had the best rebounding average (19.49).

An overwhelming selection as both Rookie of the Year and Most Valuable Player, the 6-9 Haywood capped his first year as a professional with a 59-point performance against Los Angeles. It broke the single-game ABA scoring record of 57 points set Nov. 27, 1968, by Minnesota's Connie Hawkins against the New York Nets.

Haywood also became the first player since Wilt Chamberlain to score more than 2,500 points in his rookie season. Chamberlain had 2,707 in 72 games with the Philadelphia Warriors of the National Basketball Association in 1959-60.

Haywood's total points, total rebounds and rebounding average are league records. Previously, Larry Jones of Denver held the record for total points with 2,133 and Mel Daniels of Indiana held the records for total rebounds with 1,256 and rebounding average with 16.5, all set during the 1968-69 season.

Carrier converted 454 of 509 attempts for an .892 percentage, bettering the record of .888 set by Rick Barry, then with Oakland, in 1968-69.

Carrier connected on 105 of 280 3-point field goal attempts for .375.

ABA PLAYOFFS

With 6-5 Roger Brown blazing hot, the Indiana Pacers put away the Los Angeles Stars in six games to take the 1970 ABA championship. That the Stars got to the finals was a surprise to many in the league, but Brown's 32.7 points-per-game average in the six contests and the strong rebounding-scoring of center Mel Daniels were more than L.A. could handle. Although Brown averaged 28.53 points-per-game in 15 playoff contests, high-scoring average honors went to Washington's Rick Barry, who notched an average of 40.14 in seven games, while Denver's Spencer Haywood weighed in with a 36.67 mark over 12 contests.